The Letters of the Hangeul

The Korean script is called Hangeul. It was invented by King Sejong the Great in
easy writing system that everyone could use to read and write the Korean language. Before this time, only scholars and
the ruling class could read and write. King Sejong wanted all his citizens to be literate and to have a better life. Hangeul
did just that, uniting the social classes of Korea.

The consonants (**C**) and vowels (**V**) in the charts below are combined to make syllables, just as in English. Korean
syllables are formed using the following combinations: **C + V** or **C + V + C**.

Note: There are no letters for the sounds f, v and z in Hangeul.

TRACK 1	Consonants								
Basic	ㄱ	ㄴ	ㄷ	ㄹ	ㅁ	ㅂ	ㅅ	ㅇ	ㅈ
	g or k	n	d or t	r or l	m	b or p	s or sh	ng	j or ch
Double	ㄲ		ㄸ			ㅃ	ㅆ		ㅉ
	kk		tt			pp	ss		jj
Heavy	ㅋ		ㅌ			ㅍ		ㅎ	ㅊ
	k		t			p		h	ch

TRACK 2	Vowels								
Single	ㅏ		ㅓ		ㅣ	ㅗ	ㅜ	ㅡ	
	a		eo		i	o	u	eu	
Double	ㅑ	ㅐ	ㅒ	ㅕ	ㅔ	ㅖ	ㅛ	ㅠ	
	ya	ae	yae	yeo	e	ye	yo	yu	
	ㅘ	ㅙ	ㅚ	ㅝ	ㅞ	ㅟ	ㅢ		
	wa	wae	oe	weo	we	wi	ui		

1

Simple Consonants

The list below gives the Korean consonants along with their equivalent sounds in English and some examples of these consonants as they appear within words. Note that when they are combined with vowels to create syllables and words, the shape of the simple consonants may change slightly.

Letter	Sound	Examples		
ㄱ	g or k	개미	**gaemi**	ant
		가방	**gabang**	bag
		미국	**miguk**	U.S.A.
ㄴ	n	나비	**nabi**	butterfly
		노랑	**norang**	yellow
		한국	**hanguk**	Korean
ㄷ	d or t	달	**dal**	moon
		닭	**dak**	chicken
		사다리	**sadari**	ladder
ㄹ	r or l	라디오	**ladio**	radio
		라켓	**raket**	rocket
		말	**mal**	horse
ㅁ	m	무지개	**mujigae**	rainbow
		모자	**moja**	hat
		엄마	**eomma**	mom
ㅂ	b or p	바람	**baram**	wind
		바지	**baji**	pants
		입	**ip**	lip
ㅅ	s or sh	소	**so**	cow
		사탕	**satang**	candy
		신발	**shinbal**	shoes
ㅇ	(silent) or ng*	야구	**yagu**	baseball
		여우	**yeowoo**	fox
		우산	**usan**	umbrella
ㅈ	j or ch	지구	**jigu**	earth
		의자	**uija**	chair
		주스	**juseu**	juice

*The Korean letter ㅇ is silent at the beginning of a syllable. At the end of a syllable it has the **ng** sound. If a syllable begins with a vowel, this silent consonant is written in front of the vowel as a placeholder. This is because of the rule that every syllable in Hangeul must begin with a consonant.*

Double Consonants

Hangeul has five double consonants. They have the same sound as the single consonants but are pronounced more forcefully. Double consonants are hard for English speakers to distinguish and pronounce. With a little practice though, you'll soon get the hang of it!

Letter	Sound	Examples		
ㄲ	kk	까치	kkachi	magpie
		꿈	kkum	dream
ㄸ	tt	딸	ttal	daughter
		허리띠	heoritti	belt
ㅃ	pp	빠른	ppareun	fast
		뽀뽀	ppoppo	kiss
ㅆ	ss	싸움	ssaum	fight
		썰물	sseolmul	low tide
ㅉ	jj	짜다	jjada	salty
		짧다	jjalda	short

Heavy Consonants

The next five consonants are often called "heavy" consonants, sometimes called "strong" or "aspirated" consonants. They look similar to the simple consonants except they have an extra horizontal line added that changes the sound to an aspirated sound. This means that when you pronounce the letter, you add a puff of air after the sound.

Letter	Sound	Examples		
ㅋ	k	카드	kadeu	card
		커피	keopi	coffee
ㅌ	t	토끼	tokki	rabbit
		트림	teurim	burp
ㅍ	p	피	pi	blood
		파산	pasan	bankrupt
ㅎ	h	하늘	haneul	sky
		희망	huimang	hope
ㅊ	ch	차	cha	car
		춤	chum	dance

Simple Vowels

Hangeul has six simple vowels. However, those vowels can also be doubled by writing them twice side by side or on top of each other or combined with other vowels to create up to 21 different vowel sounds. Remember that a vowel (**V**) is always combined with a consonant (**C**) to make a syllable in one of the following combinations: **C + V** or **C + V + C** (also written **CV** and **CVC**). There are two types of simple vowel: vertical vowels, written to the right of the consonant, and horizontal vowels, written underneath the consonant.

Vertical Vowels

Vertical vowels are always written to the right of the consonant.

Letter	Sound		Examples		
ㅏ	a	sounds like the vowel **a** in *lalala*	아침	achim	breakfast
			아들	adeul	son
ㅓ	eo	sounds like the vowel **u** in *run*	얼음	eoreum	ice
			어제	eoje	yesterday
ㅣ	i	sounds like **ee** in *jeep*	이름	ireum	name
			이불	ibul	blanket

Horizontal Vowels

Horizontal vowels are always written underneath the consonant.

Letter	Sound		Examples		
ㅗ	o	sounds like the vowel **o** in *Joe*	오리	ori	duck
			오이	oi	cucumber
ㅜ	u	sounds like the vowel **u** in *June*	우유	uyu	milk
			우산	usan	umbrella
ㅡ	eu	sounds like the vowel **u** in *push*	은행	eunhaeng	bank
			음식	eumsik	food

Double Vertical Vowels

Adding an extra line to a simple vowel, or combining two simple vowels, creates a new sound. This combination of two vowel sounds to make a single new sound is called a diphthong in English.

Letter	Sound		Examples		
ㅑ	ya	sounds like **ya** in *yahoo*	양말	yangmal	socks
			야구	yagu	baseball
ㅕ	yeo	sounds like **you** in *young*	연	yeon	kite
			여자	yeoja	woman

Letter	Sound		Examples		
ㅔ	e	sounds like **e** in *let*	에너지	eneoji	energy
			엔진	enjin	engine
ㅐ	ae	sounds like **e** in *let*	애칭	aeching	nickname
			애국자	aegukja	patriot
ㅒ	yae	sounds like **ye** in *yes*	얘기	yaegi	story
			얘들아	yaedeula	guys
ㅖ	ye	sounds like **ye** in *yes*	예약	yeyak	reservation
			예의	yeui	etiquette

Double Horizontal Vowels

Letter	Sound		Examples		
ㅛ	yo	sounds like **yo** in *yogurt*	요구	yogu	demand
			요술	yosul	magic
ㅠ	yu	sounds like **yu** in *yuletide*	유행	yuhaeng	trend
			유명	yumyeong	famous

Combined Horizontal and Vertical Vowels

These letters consist of two vowels combined to make a new sound, also known as a diphthong.

Letter	Sound		Examples		
ㅘ	wa	sounds like **wa** in *watch*	와인	wain	wine
			완벽	wanbyeok	perfect
ㅙ	wae	sounds like **we** in *wed*	왜곡	waegok	distortion
			왜소	waeso	small
ㅚ	oe	sounds like **we** in *wet*	외모	oemo	appearance
			외식	oesik	eat out
ㅝ	weo	sounds like **wo** in *worry*	원리	weonri	principle
			원인	weonin	cause
ㅞ	we	sounds like **we** in *wet*	웨이터	weiteo	waiter
			웨딩	weding	wedding
ㅟ	wi	sounds like the **wee** in *weed*	위치	wichi	location
			위조	wijo	forge
ㅢ	ui	sounds like the **u** in *push* and the **ee** in *sleep*, combined	의심	uisim	doubt
			의자	uija	chair

Practice Writing Hangeul Letters

Forming the letters of Korean alphabet is easy! There are just two basic rules: horizontal strokes are written from left to right and vertical strokes are written from top to bottom, just as in English.

Let's write the consonants:

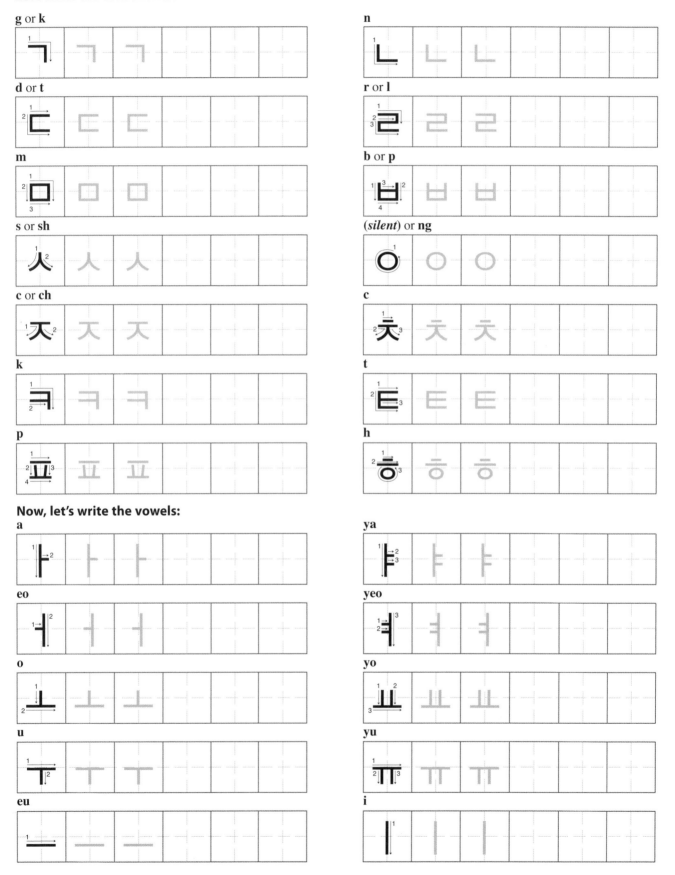

g or k

d or t

m

s or sh

c or ch

k

p

n

r or l

b or p

(*silent*) or ng

c

t

h

Now, let's write the vowels:

a

eo

o

u

eu

ya

yeo

yo

yu

i

Practice Writing Korean Syllables

Consonant + Vertical Vowel

The vertical vowels ㅏ, ㅓ and ㅣ are written to the right of the consonant, as in the following examples.

Consonant + Horizontal Vowel

Horizontal vowels ㅗ, ㅜ and ㅡ are written under the consonant, as in the following examples.

Double Consonant + Single Vowel

Write the double consonant first. If the vowel is vertical, write it on the right. If the vowel is horizontal, write it underneath.

Double Consonant + Double Vowel

Write the double consonant first. If the vowel is vertical, write it on the right. If the vowel is horizontal, write it underneath.

Heavy Consonant + Single or Double Vowel

The heavy consonants (k, t, p and h) are pronounced with a breath of air. Write the consonant first. If the vowel is vertical, write it to the right of the consonant. If the vowel is horizontal, write it underneath.

Consonant + Vowel + Consonant (CVC)

In a CVC syllable, the final consonant is written under the vowel. (Sometimes this pattern has two final consonants as in the last two examples below.)

Practice Writing Korean Words

Hangeul words can have one, two or three syllables.

소 **so** cow

차 **cha** car

피 **pi** blood

달 **dal** moon

말 **mal** horse

꿈 **kkum** dream

딸 **ttal** daughter

공 **gong** ball

돈 **don** money

불 **bul** fire

바지 **baji** pants

병원 **byeongwon** hospital

공룡 **gongryong** dinosaur

짧다 **jjalda** short

양말 **yangmal** socks

칫솔 **chitsol** toothbrush

사탕 **satang** candy

우산 **usan** umbrella

엄마 **eomma** mom

수박 **subak** watermelon

야구 **yagu** baseball

여우 **yeowoo** fox

8

주스 **juseu** juice

주	스	ㅈ	주	ㅅ	스

버스 **beoseu** bus

버	스	ㅂ	버	ㅅ	스

초코 **choco** chocolate

초	코	ㅊ	초	ㅋ	코

뽀뽀 **ppoppo** kiss

뽀	뽀	ㅃ	뽀	ㅃ	뽀

나비 **nabi** butterfly

나	비	ㄴ	나	ㅂ	비

나무 **namu** tree

나	무	ㄴ	나	ㅁ	무

어머니 **eomeoni** mother

어	머	니	ㅇ	어	ㅁ	머	ㄴ	니

아버지 **abeoji** father

아	버	지	ㅇ	아	ㅂ	버	ㅈ	지

라디오 **ladio** radio

라	디	오	ㄹ	라	ㄷ	디	ㅇ	오

자전거 **jajeongeo** bicycle

자	전	거	ㅈ	자	ㅈ	저	전	ㄱ	거

웨이터 **weiteo** waiter

웨	이	터	ㅇ	우	웨	ㅇ	이	ㅌ	터

호랑이 **horangi** tiger

호	랑	이	ㅎ	호	ㄹ	라	랑	ㅇ	이

금요일 **geumyoil** Friday

금	요	일	ㄱ	그	금	ㅇ	요	ㅇ	이	일

귀엽다 **gwiyeopda** cute

귀	엽	다	ㄱ	구	귀	ㅇ	여	엽	ㄷ	다

강하다 **ganghada** strong

강	하	다	ㄱ	가	강	ㅎ	ㅎ	하	ㄷ	다

Practice Writing Korean Phrases

안녕하세요　**annyeong haseyo**　hello

안 녕 하 세 요

환영합니다　**hwanyeonghapnida**　welcome

환 영 합 니 다

들어오세요　**deureooseyo**　please come in

들 어 오 세 요

잘 지냈어요?　**jal jinaesseoyo?**　how have you been?

잘 지 냈 어 요

잘 지냈어요　**jal jinaesseoyo**　I've been well

잘 지 냈 어 요

괜찮습니다　**gwaenchanseupnida**　it's ok

괜 찮 습 니 다

감사합니다　**gamsahapnida**　thank you

감 사 합 니 다

실례합니다　**sillyehapnida**　excuse me

실 례 합 니 다

죄송합니다　**joesonghapnida**　I am sorry

죄 송 합 니 다

안녕히 가세요　**annyeonghi gaseyo**　goodbye (to person leaving)

안 녕 히 가 세 요

안녕히 계세요　**annyeonghi gyeseyo**　goodbye (to person staying)

안 녕 히 계 세 요

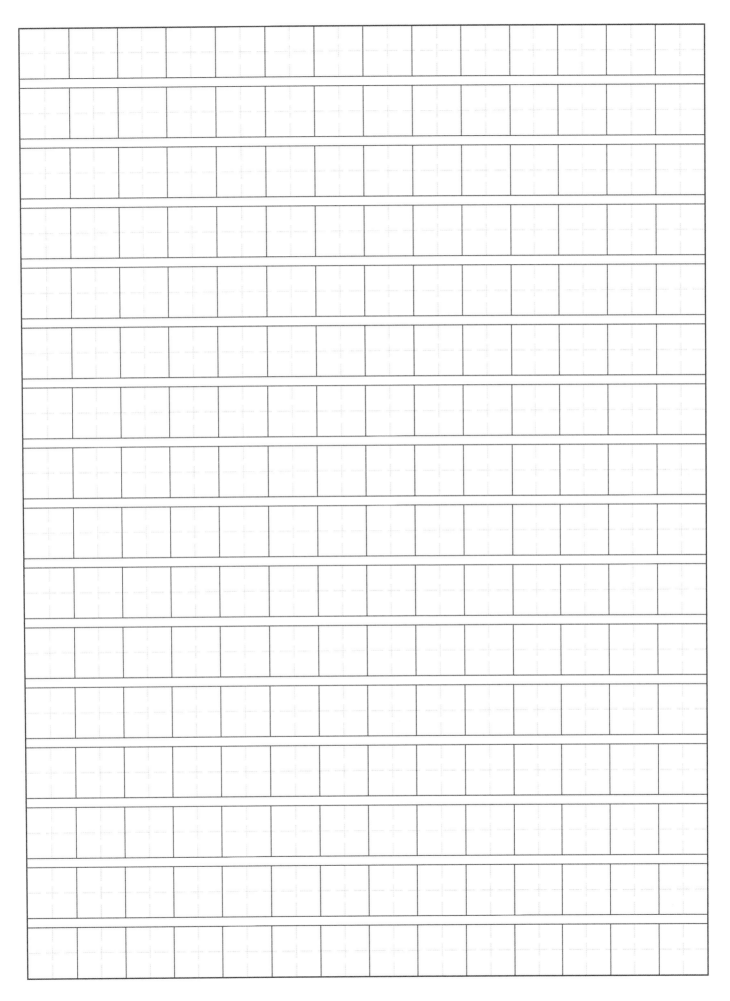

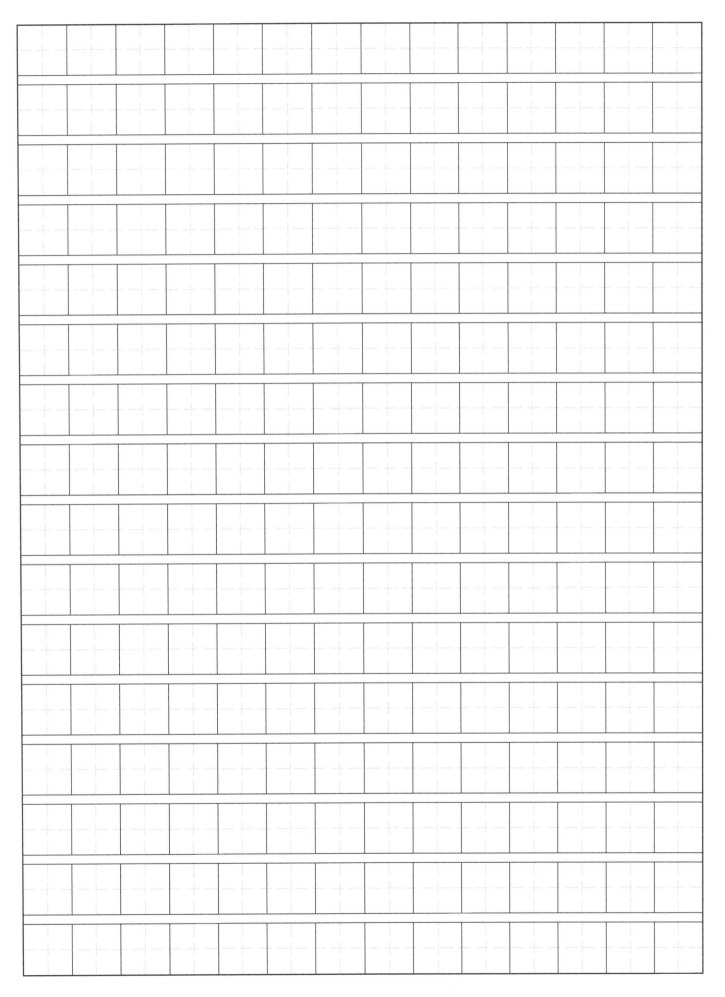

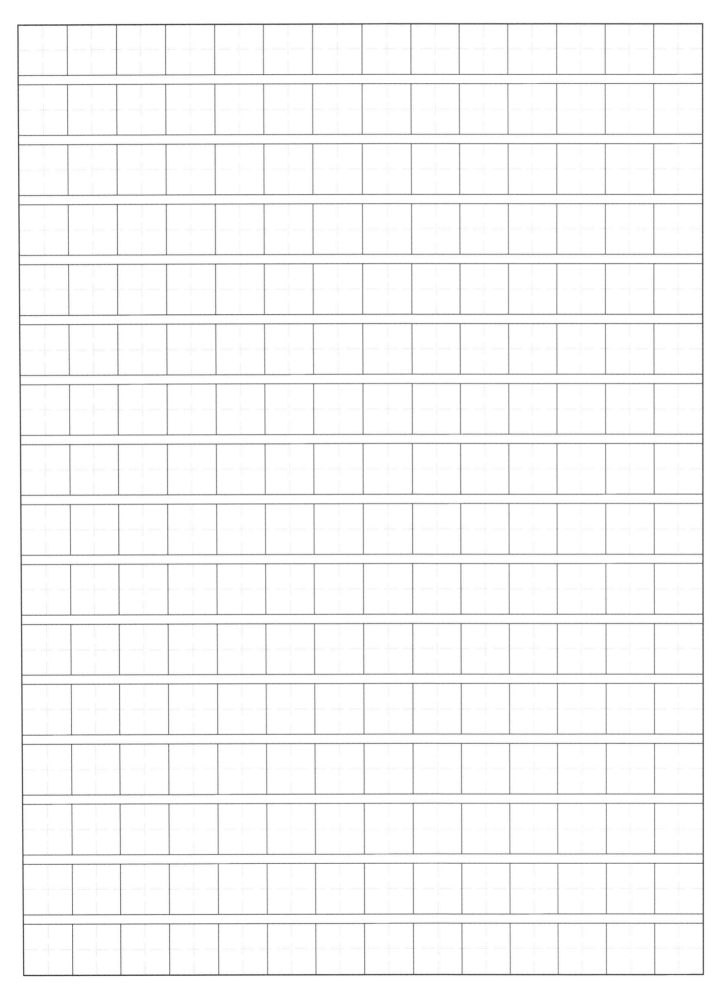

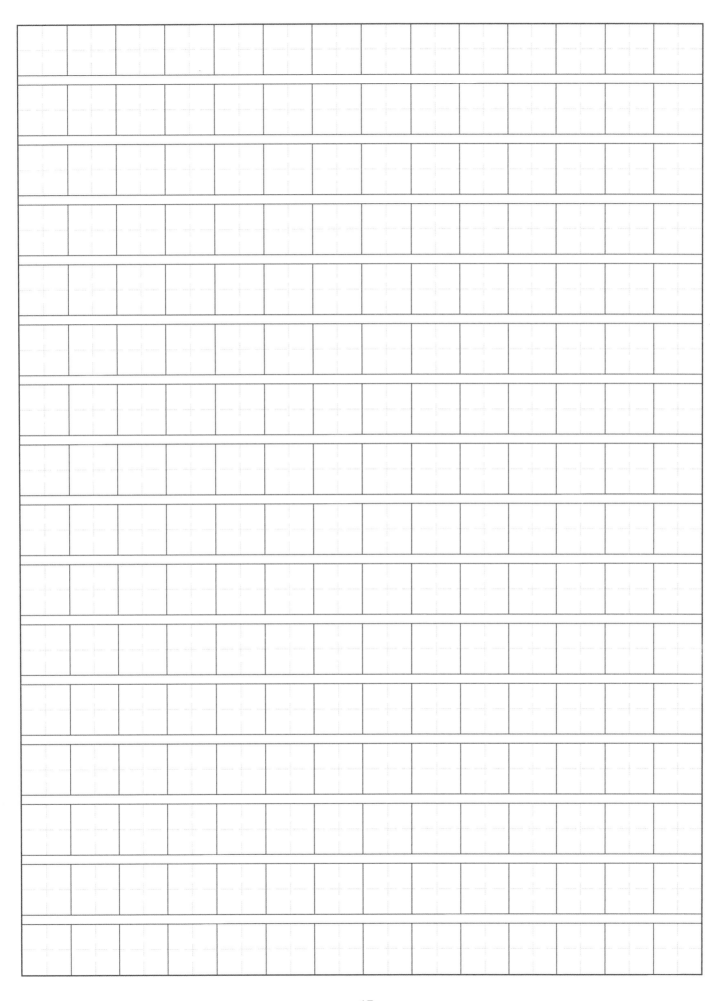

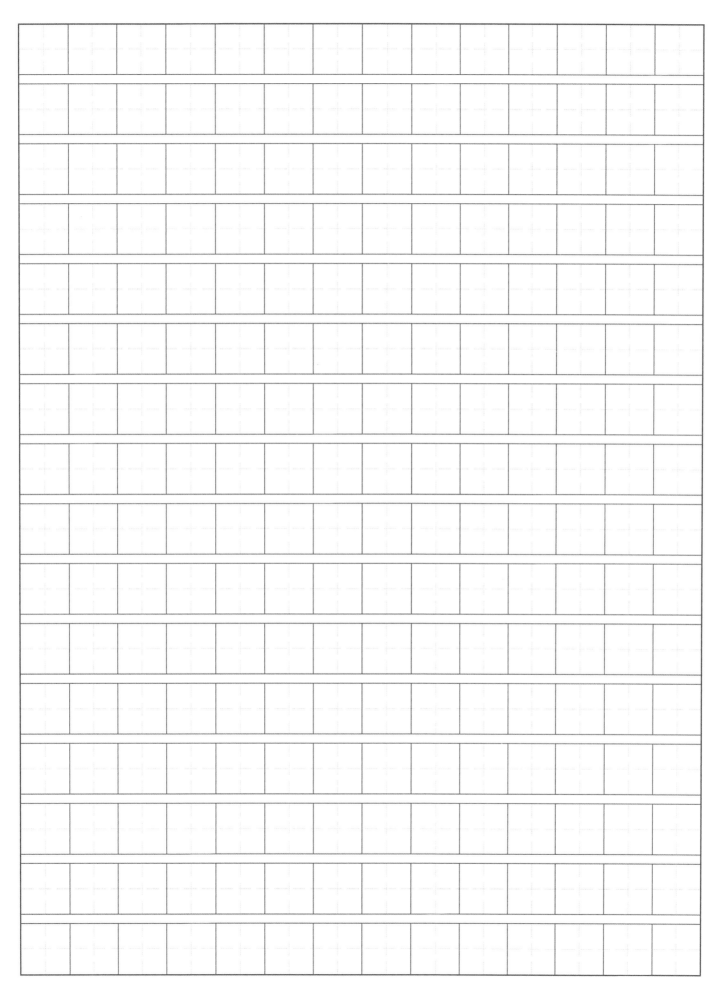

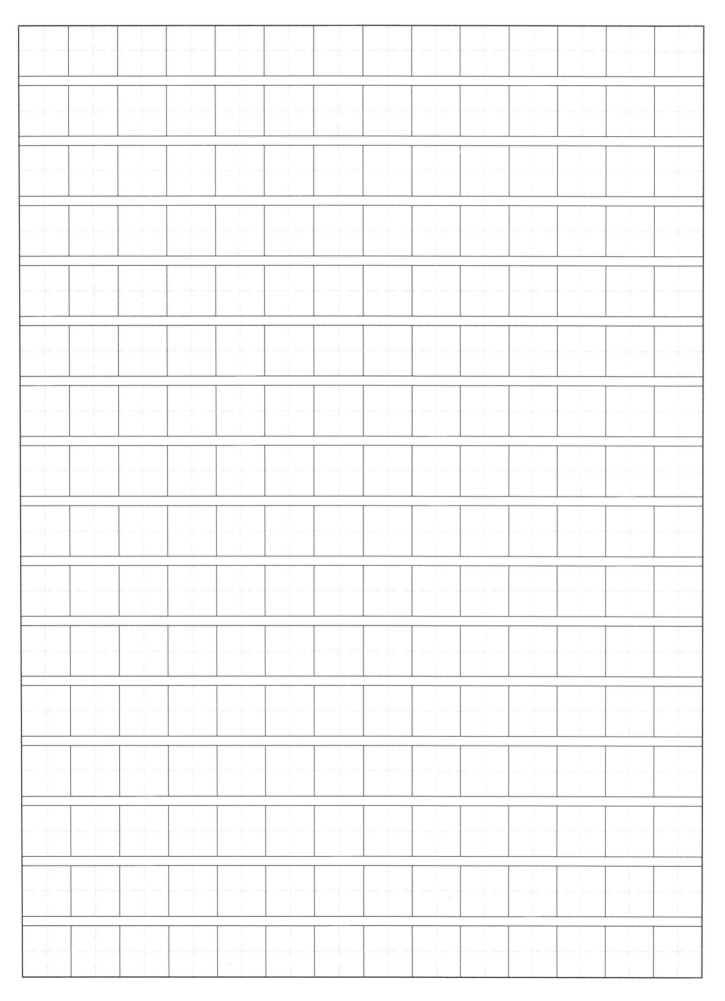

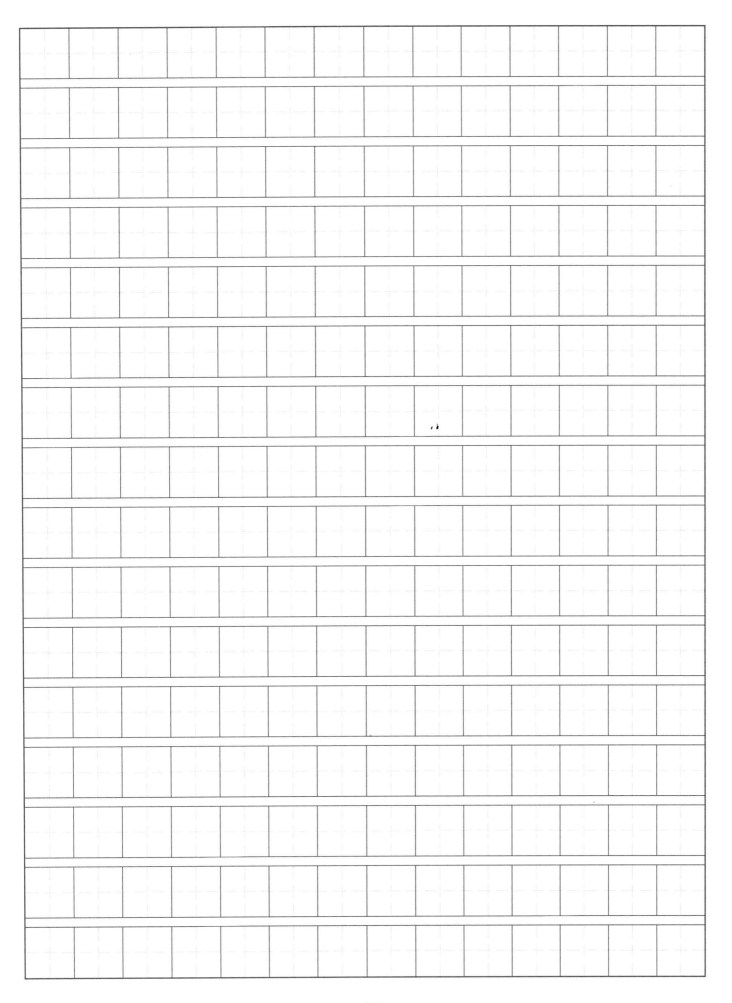

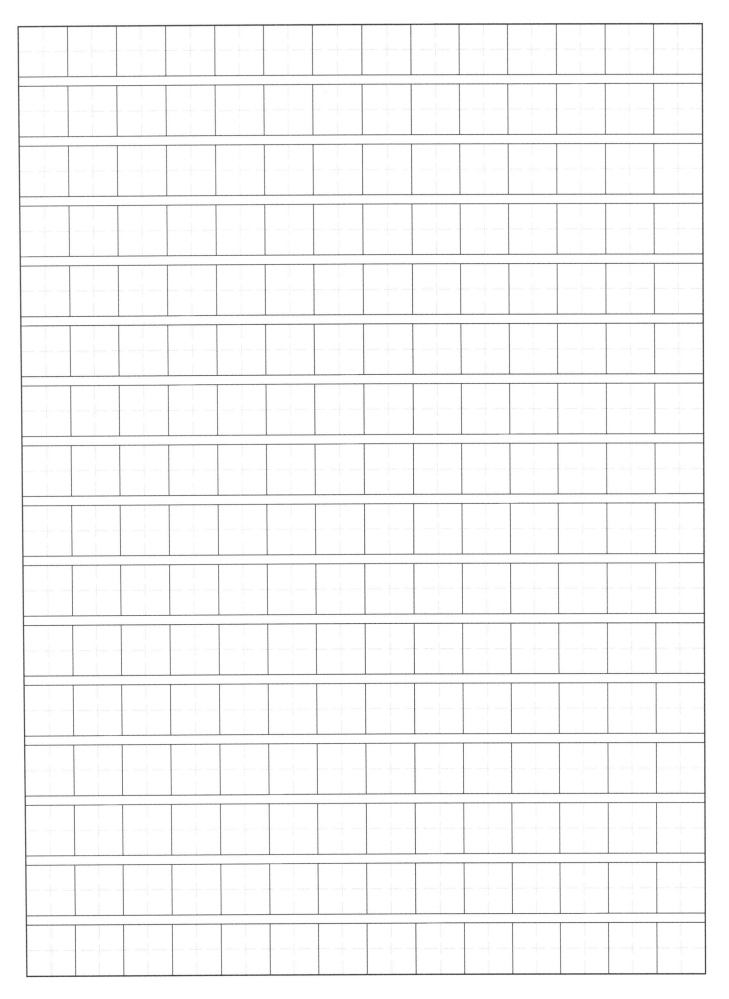

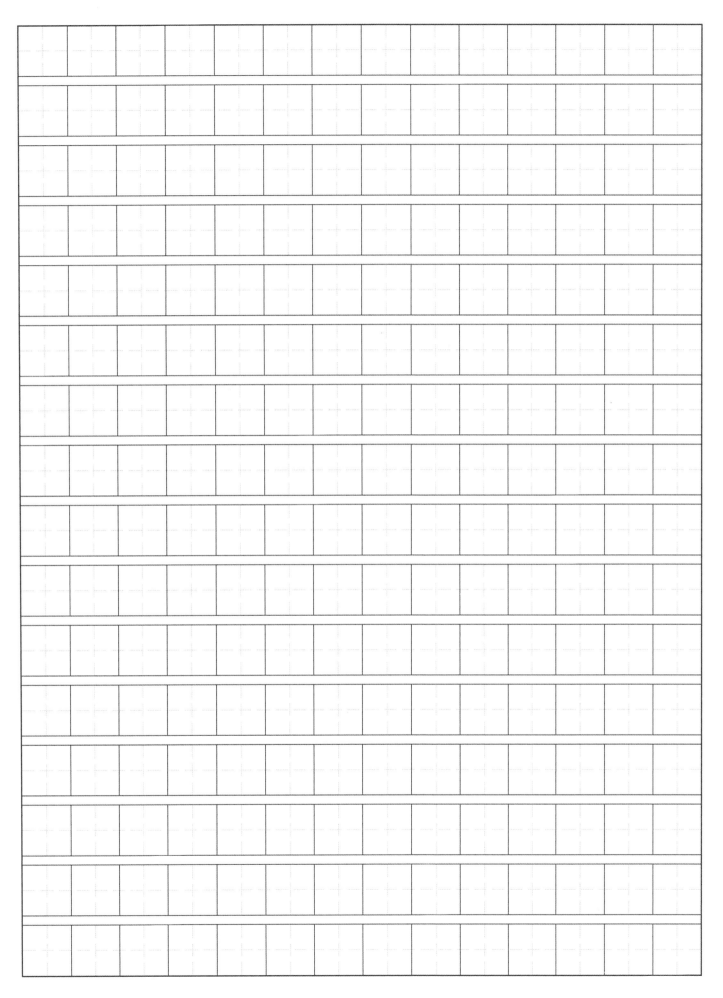

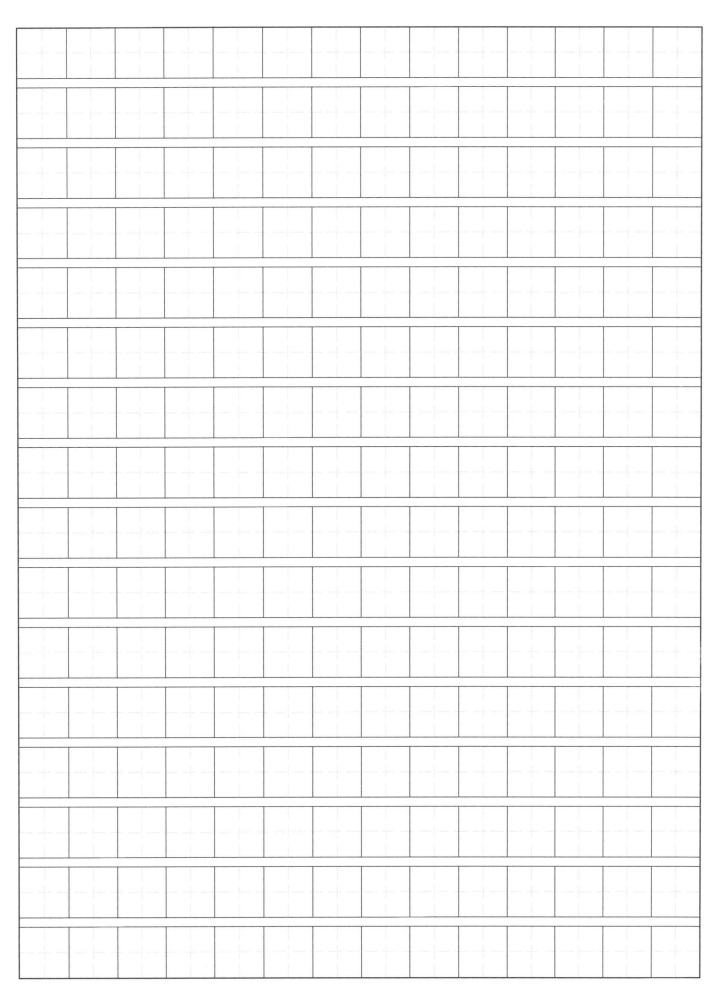

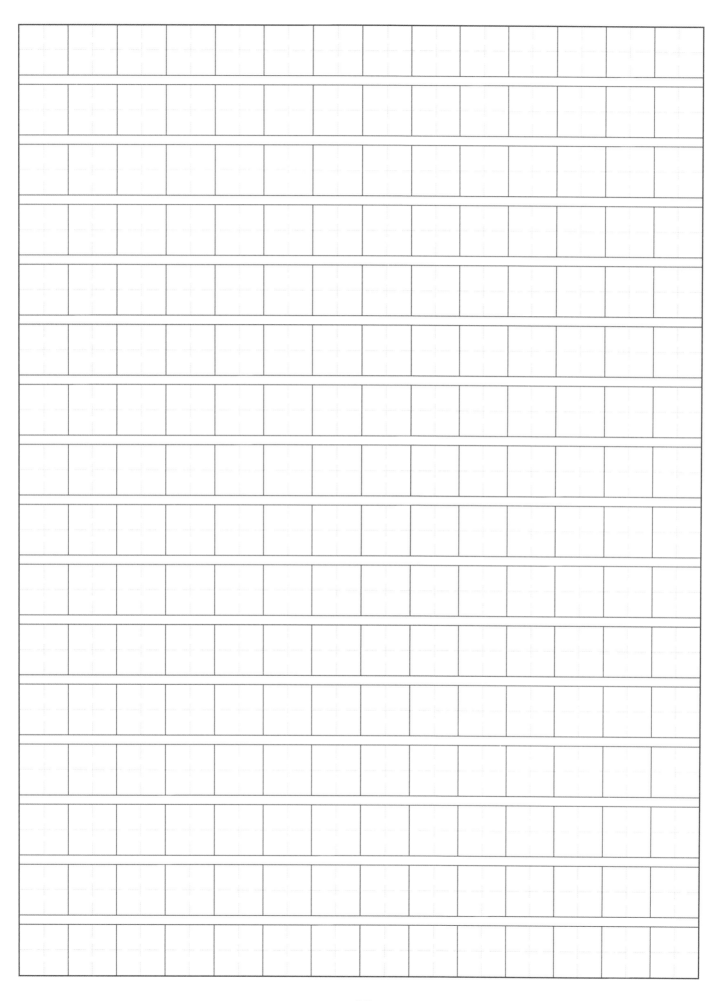

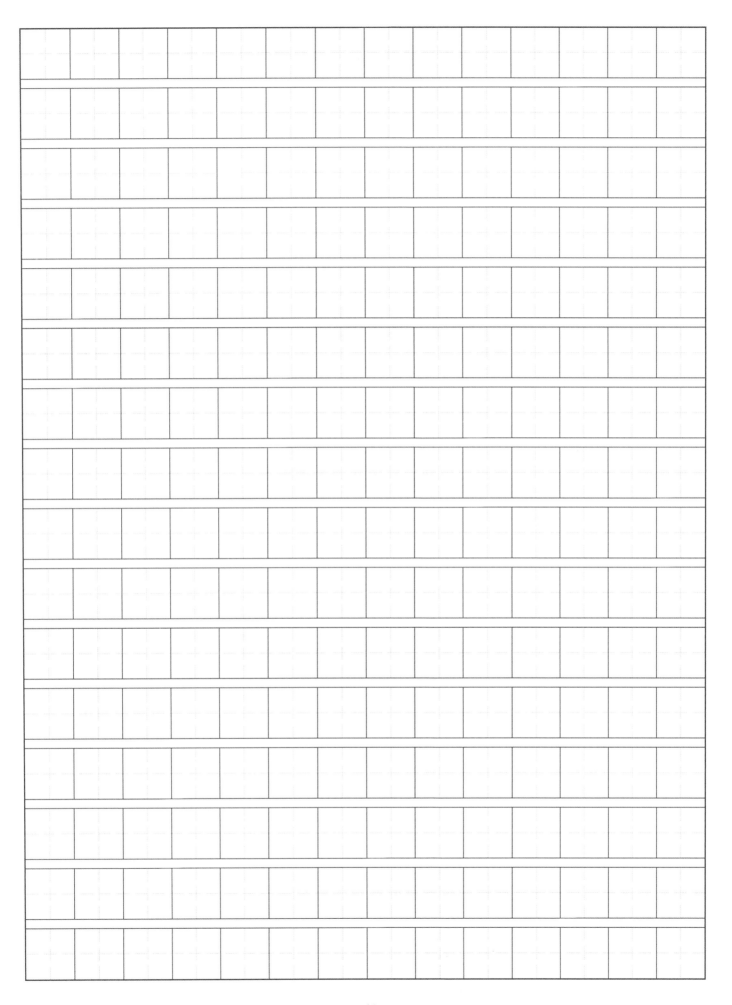

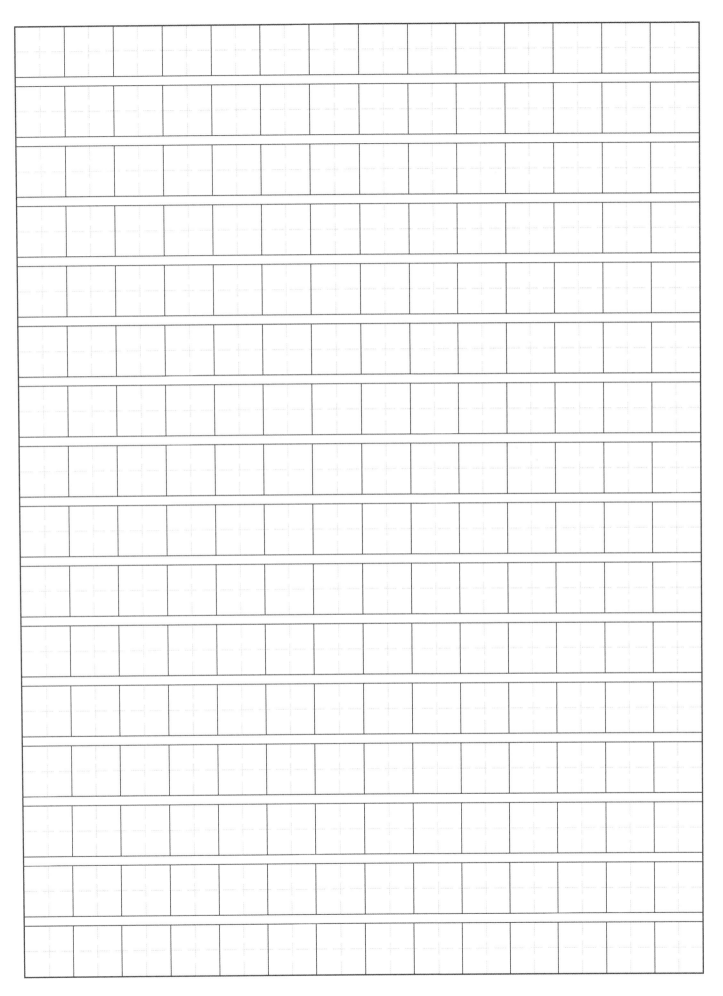

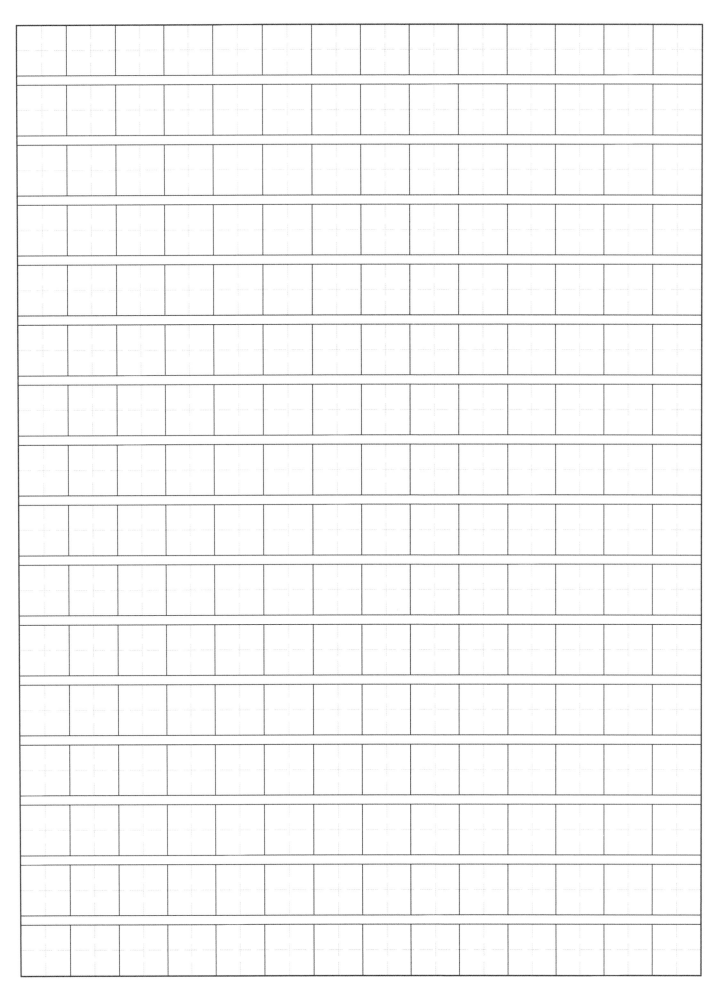

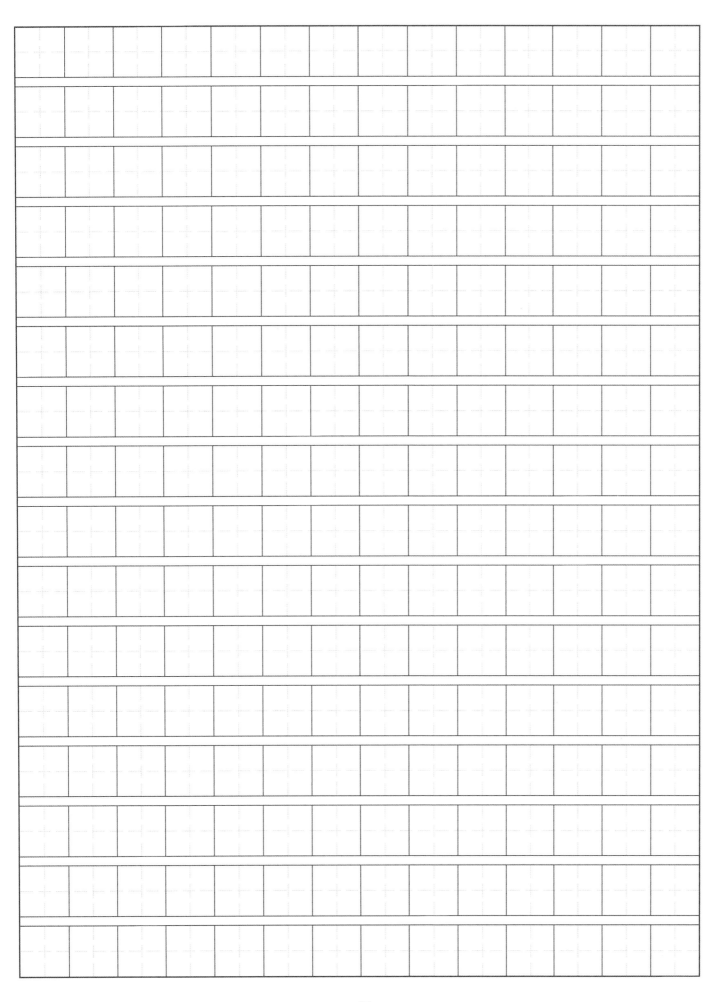

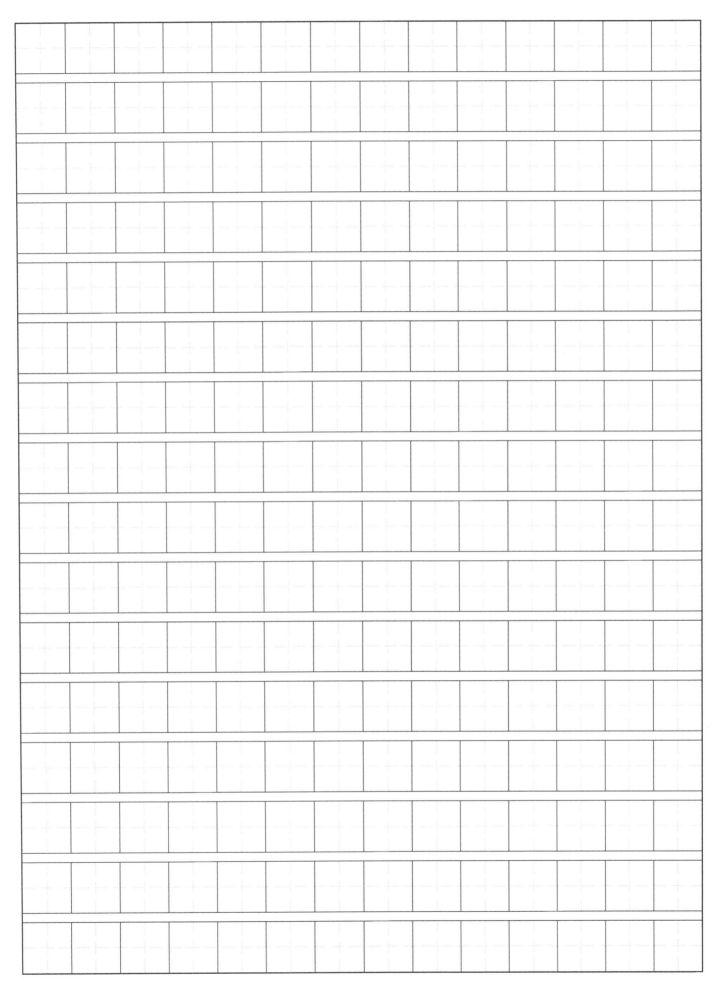

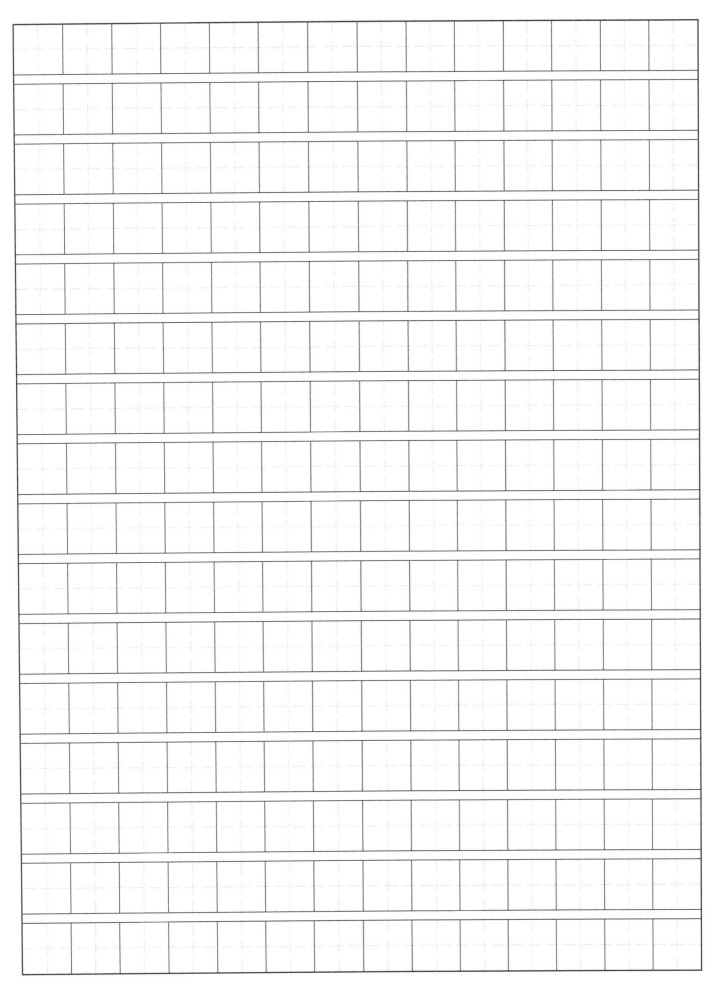

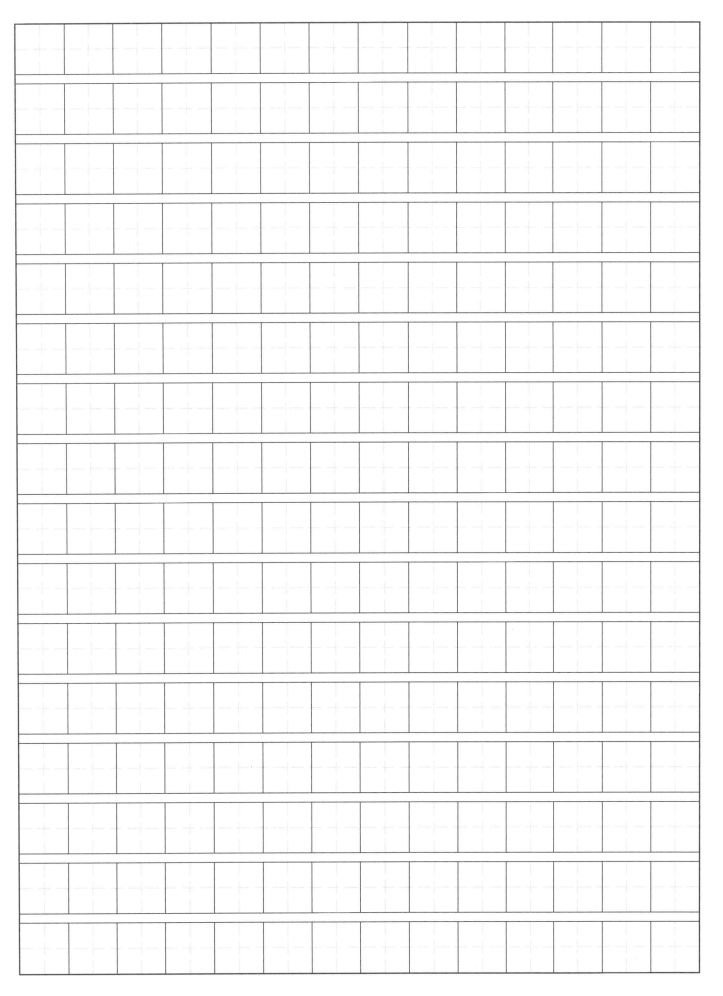

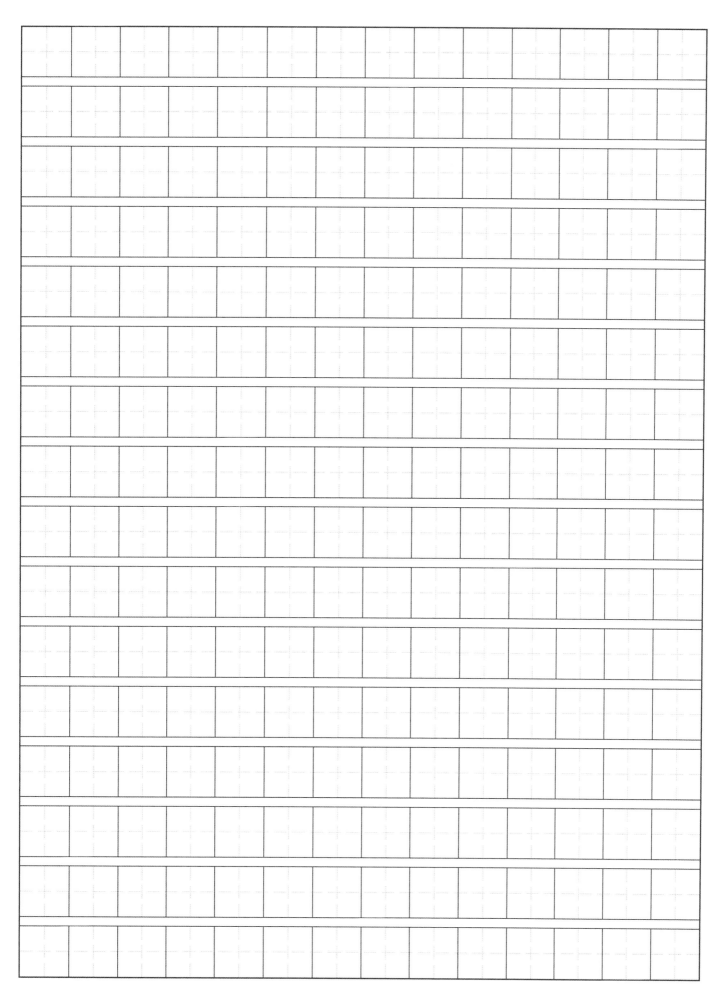

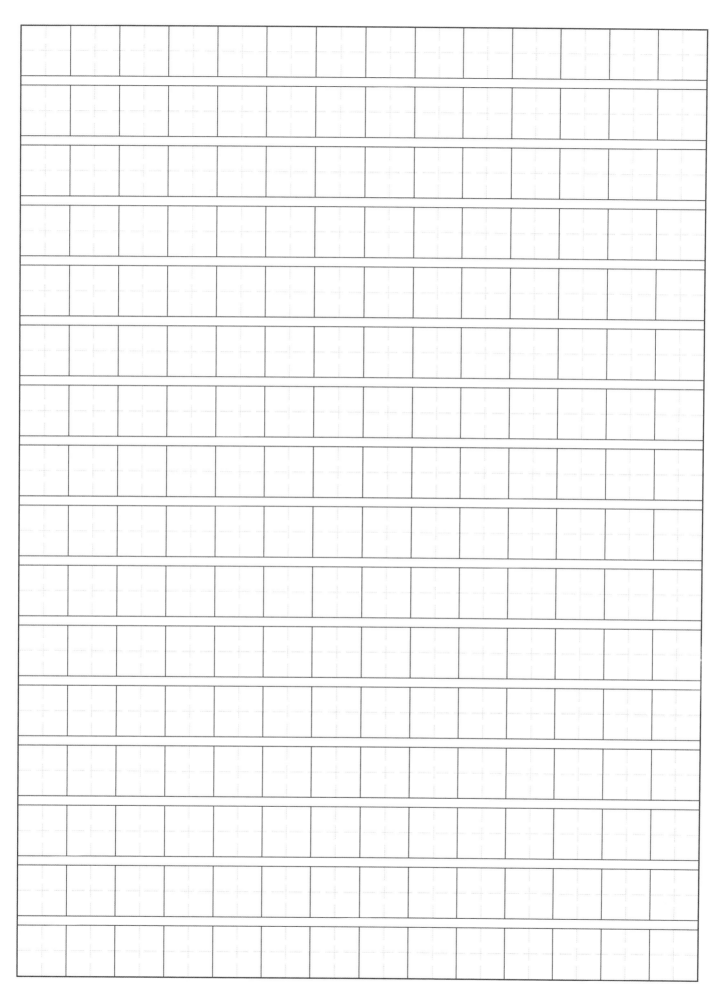

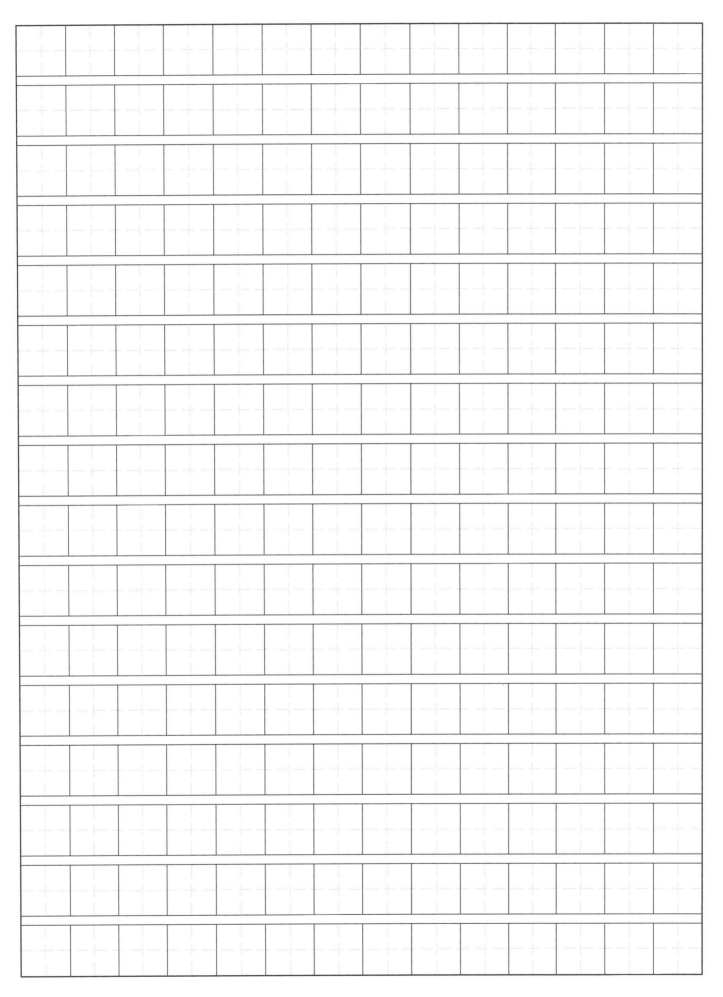

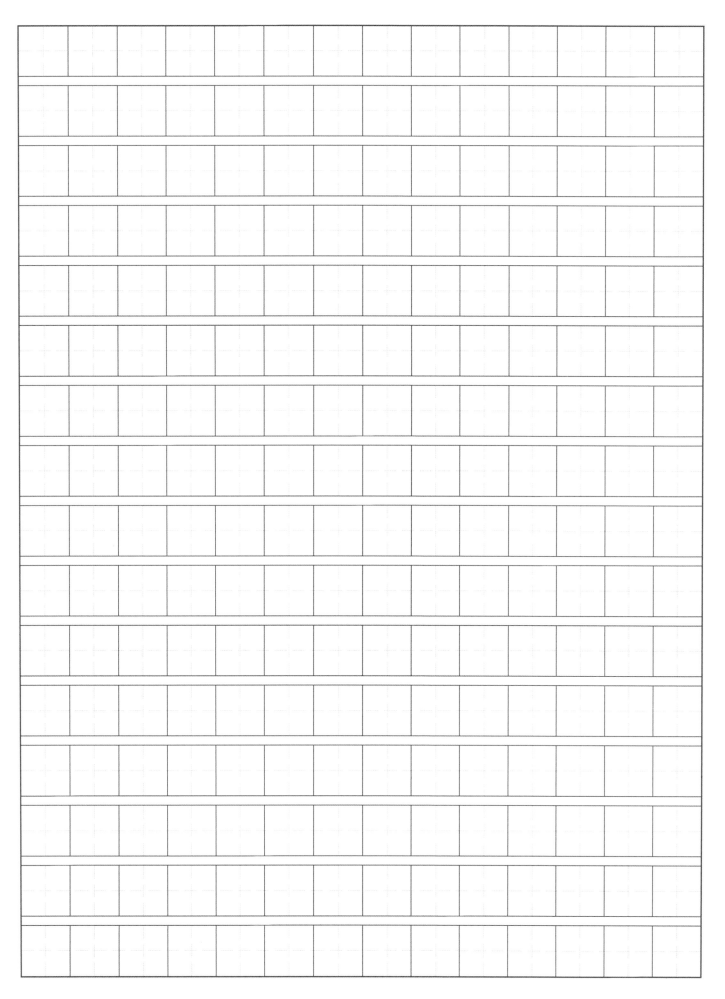

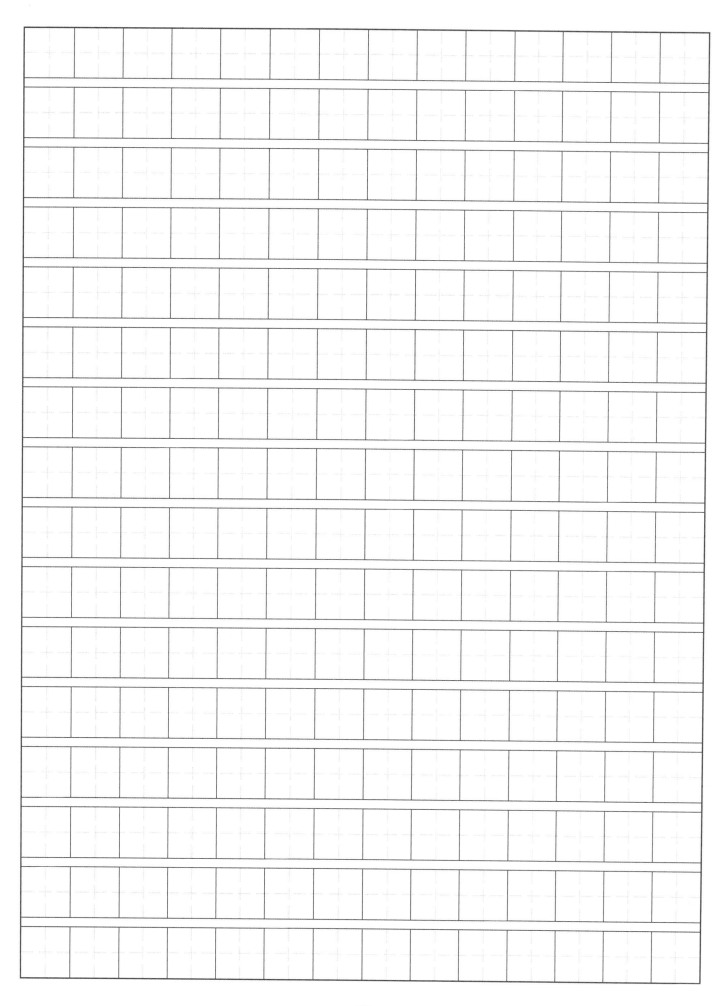

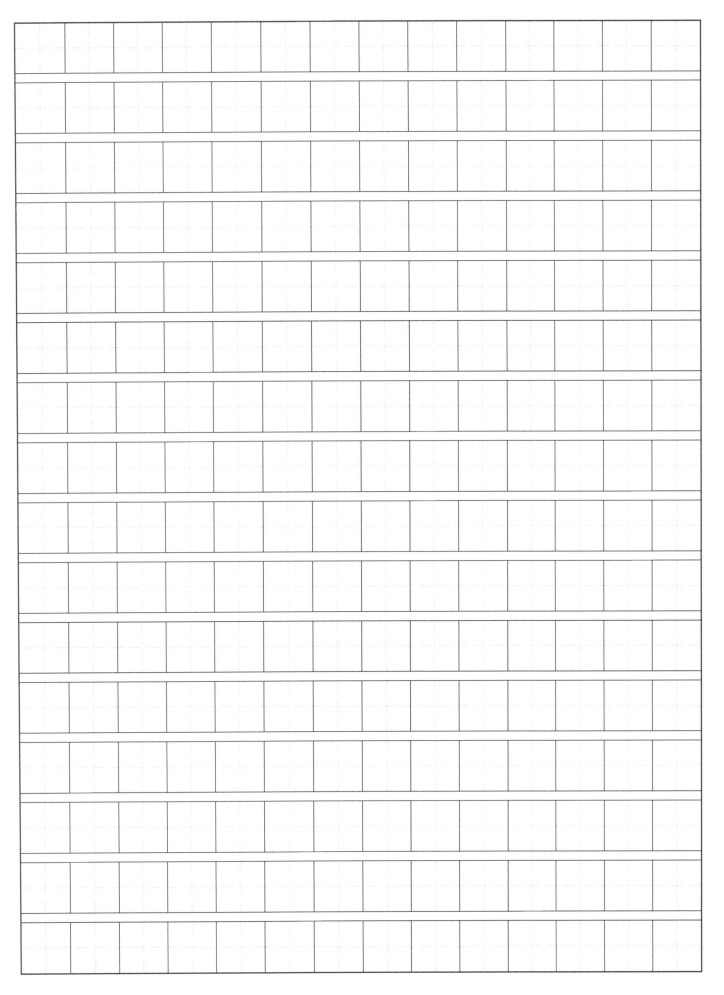

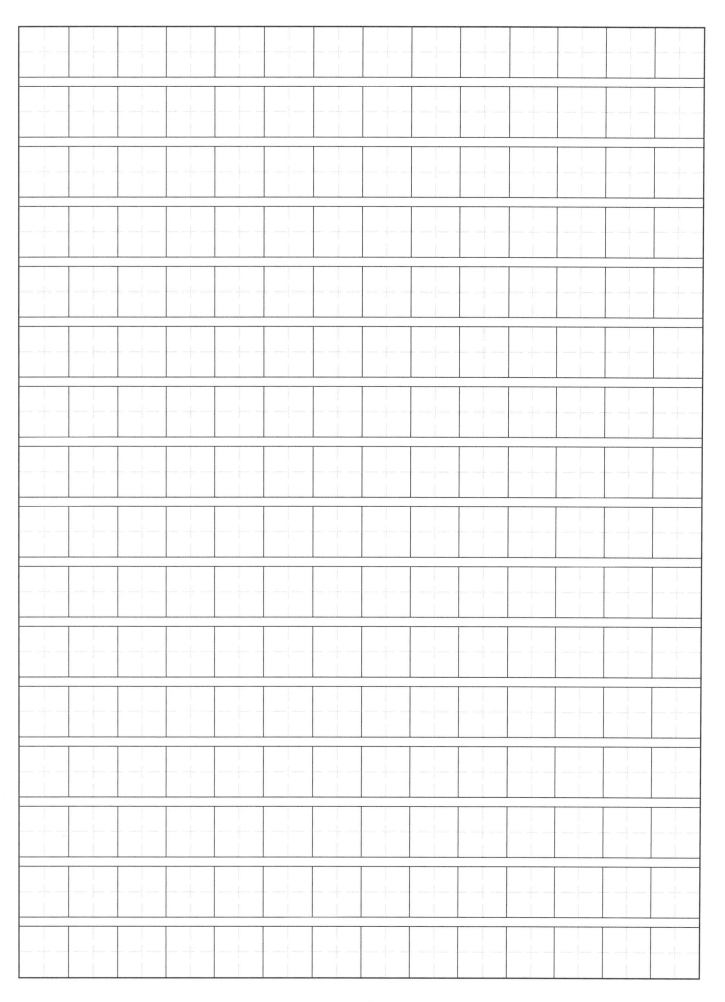

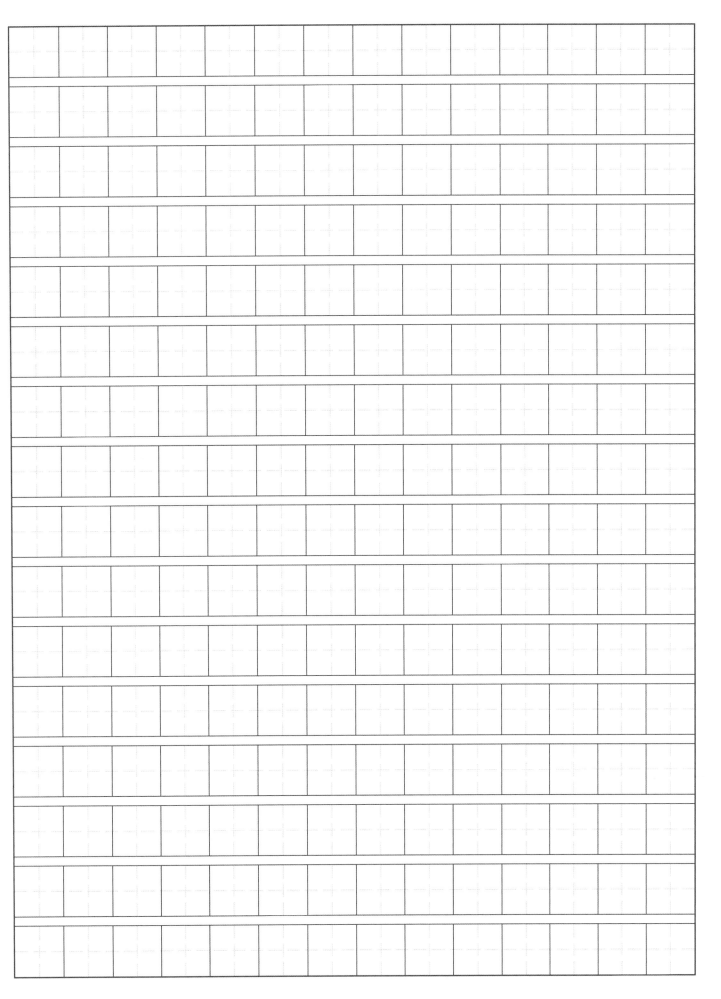

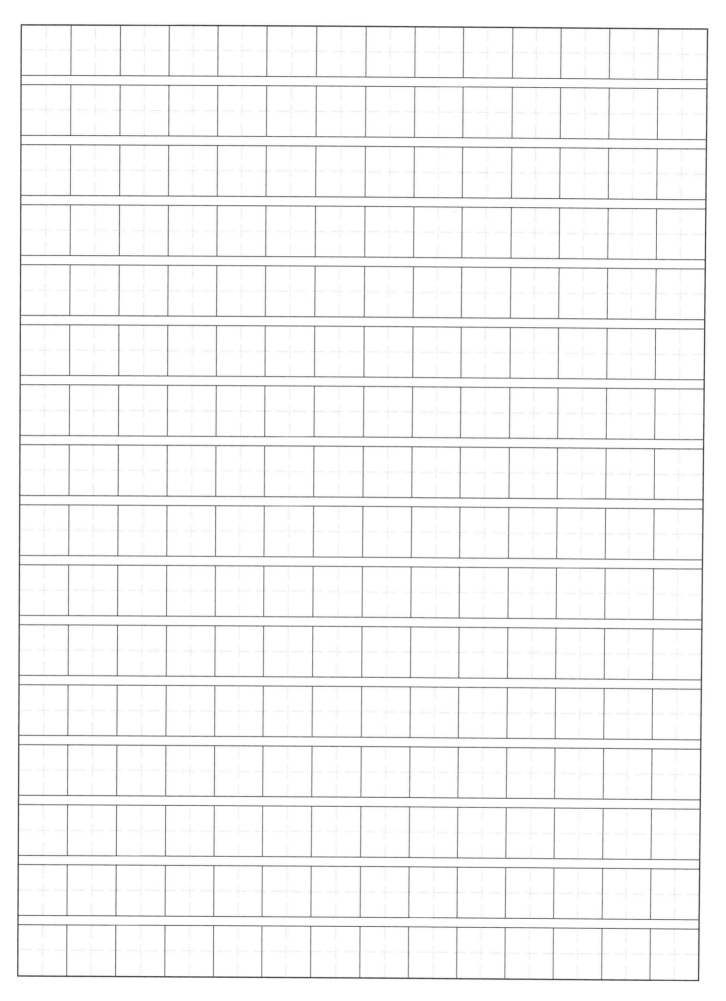

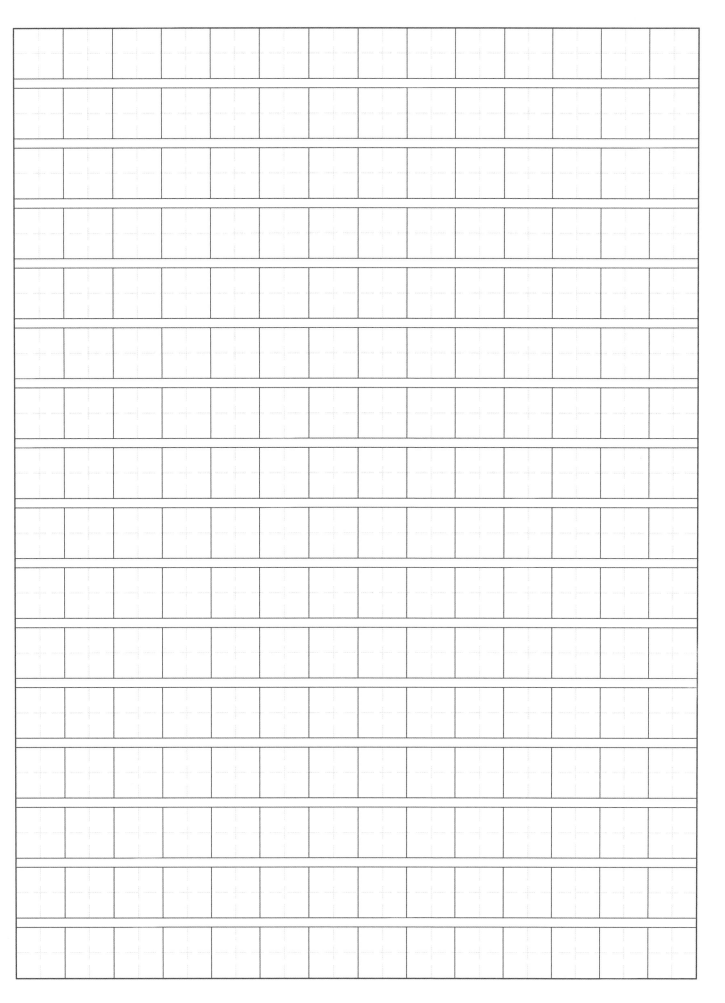

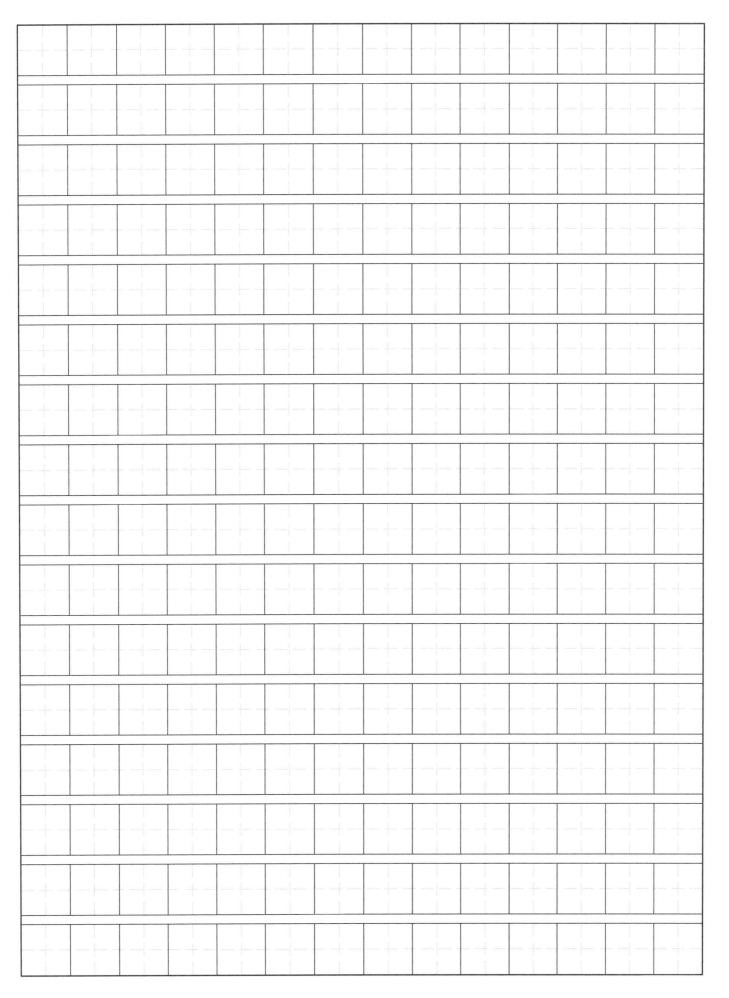

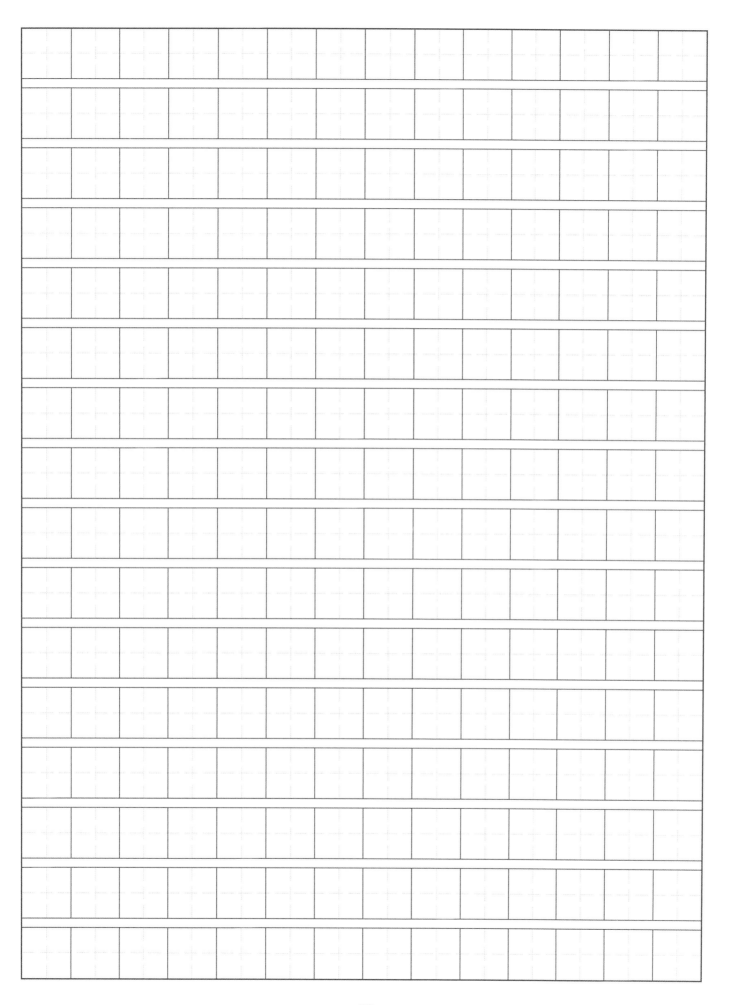

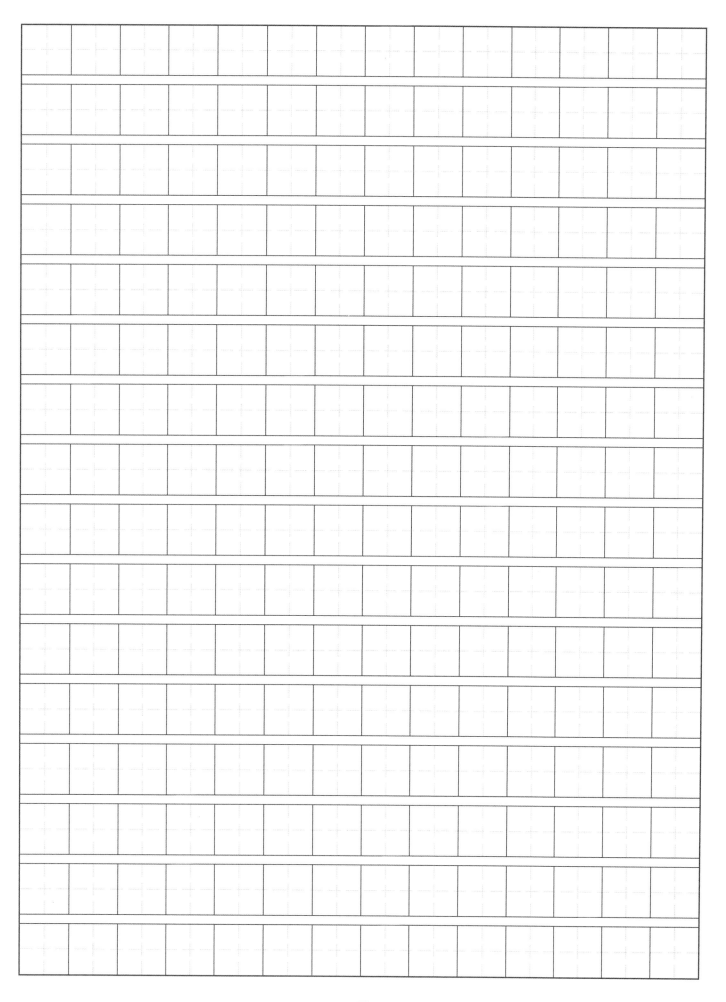

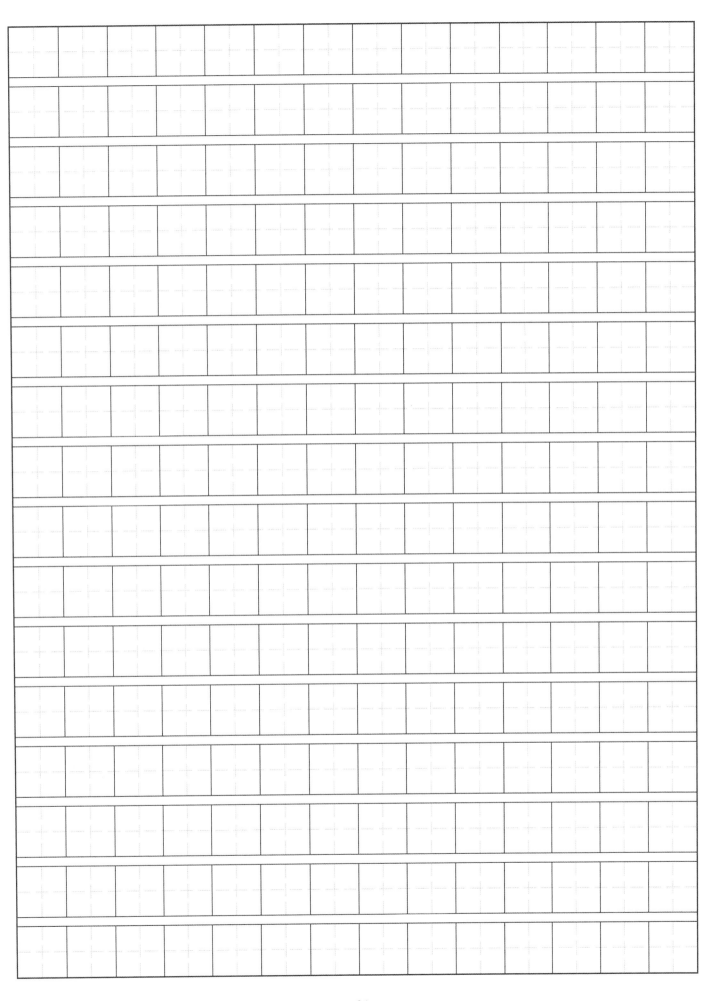

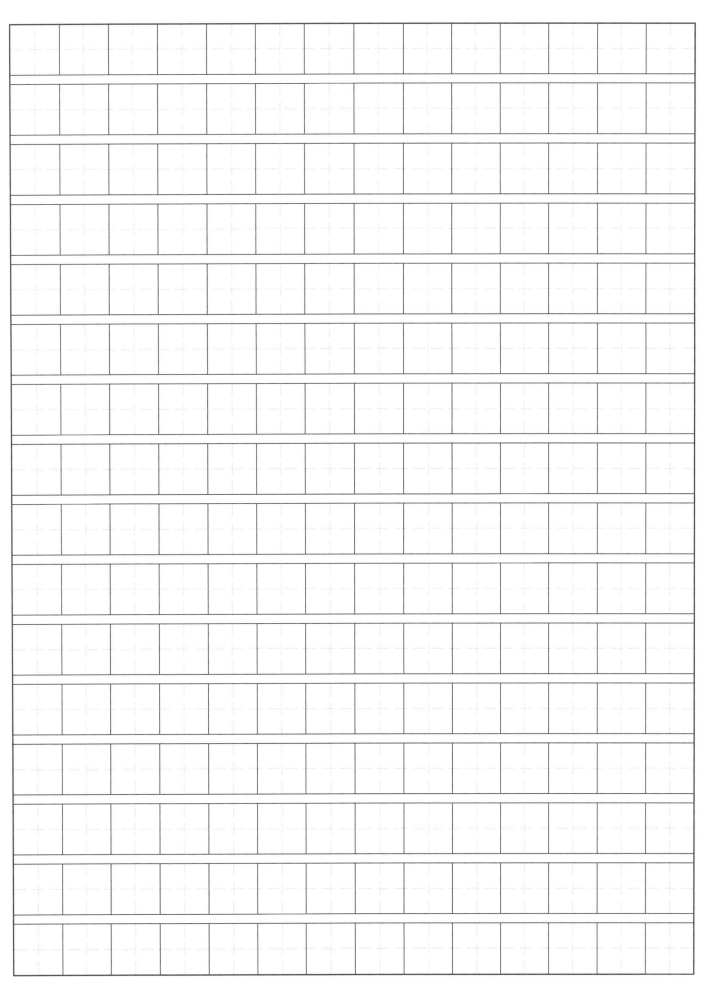

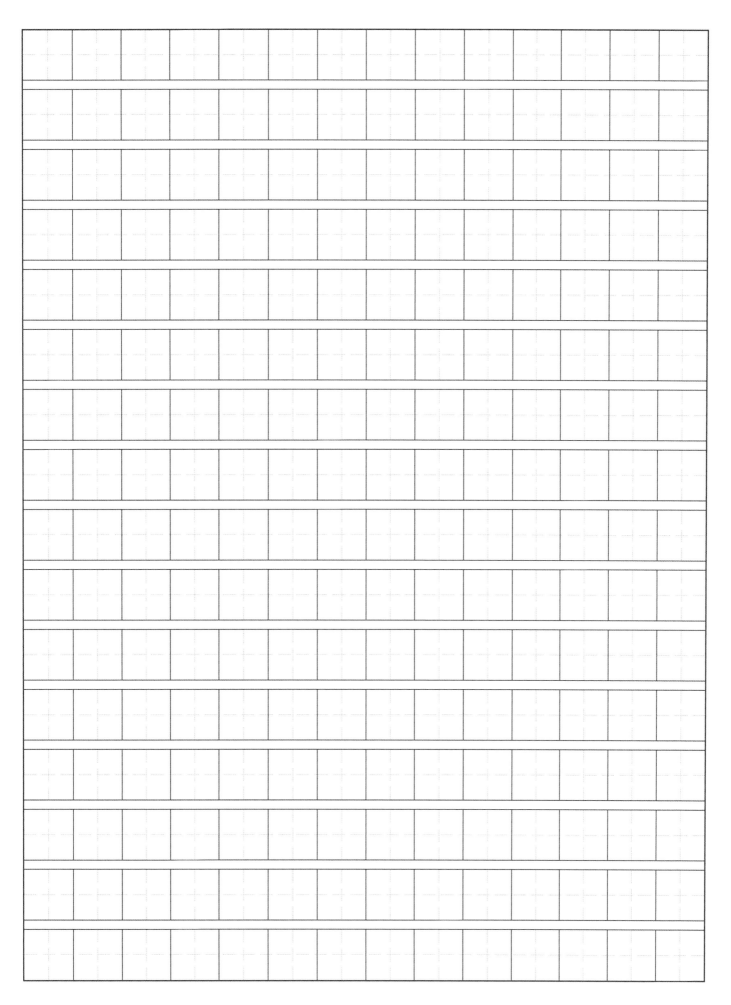

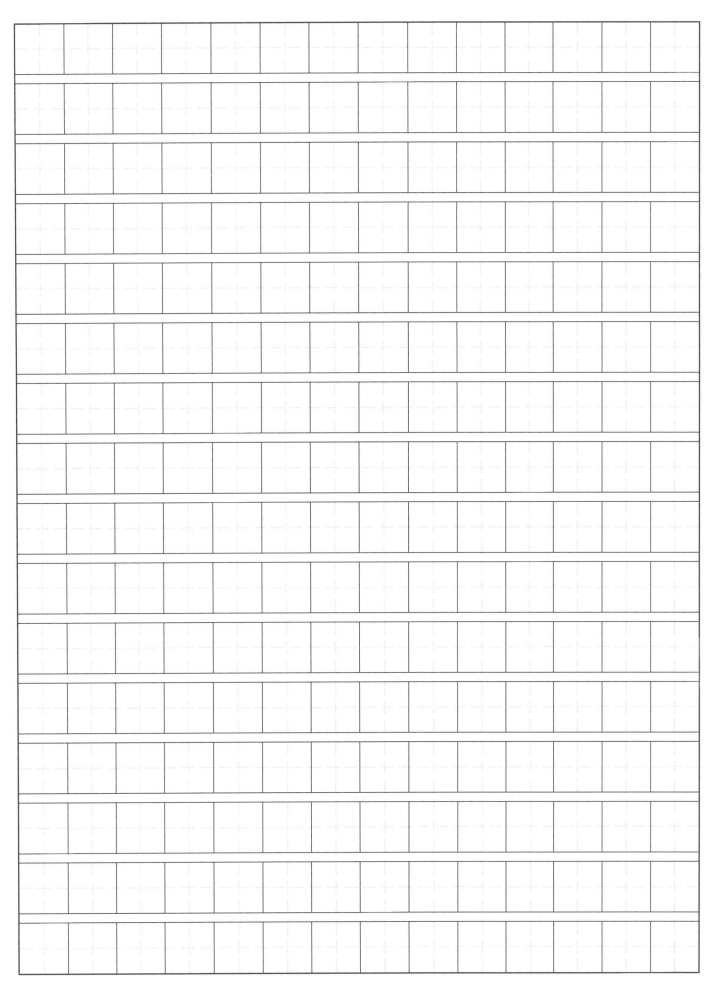

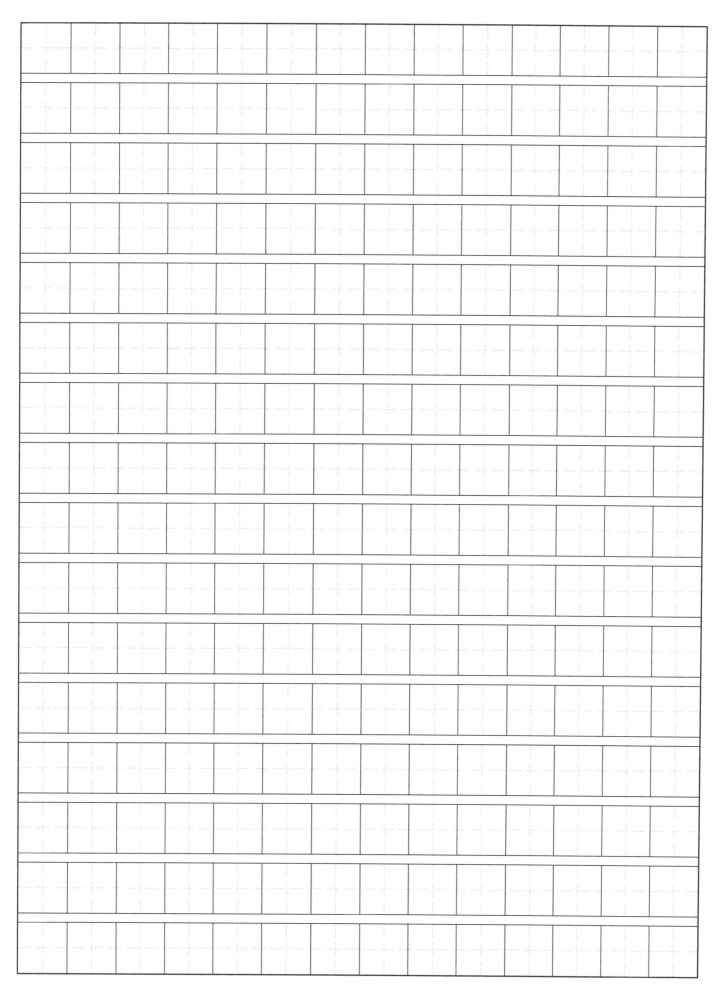

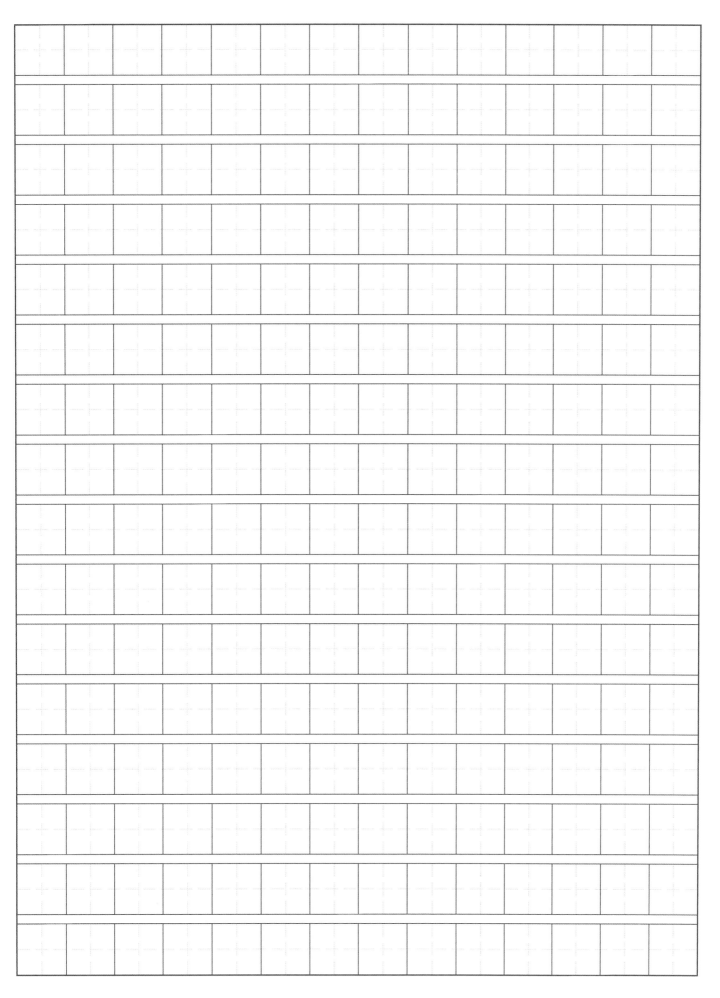

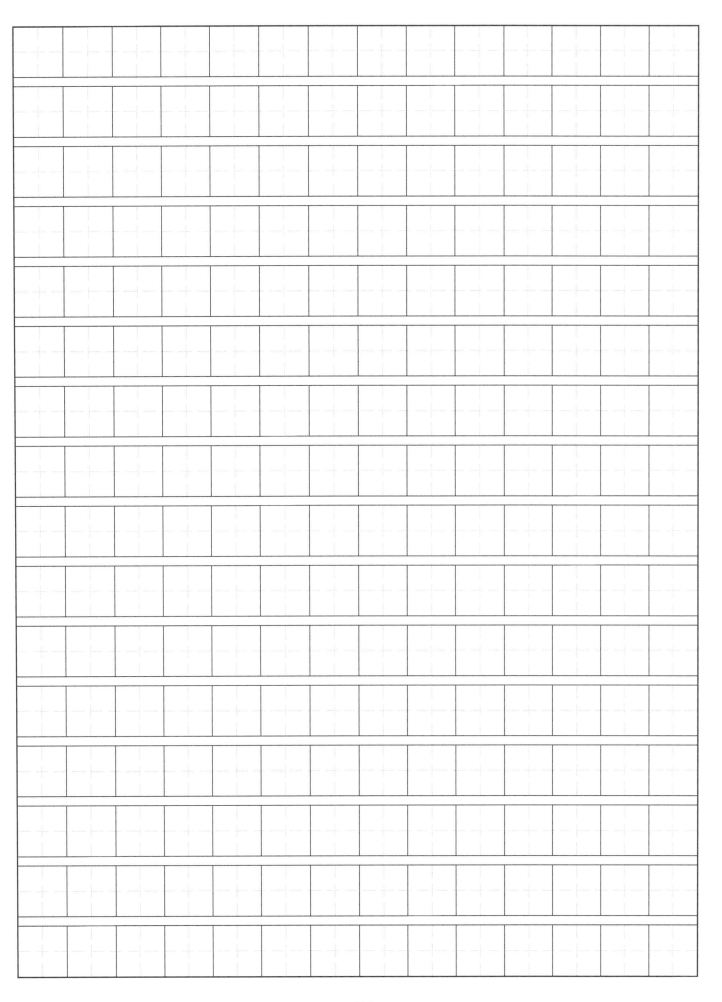

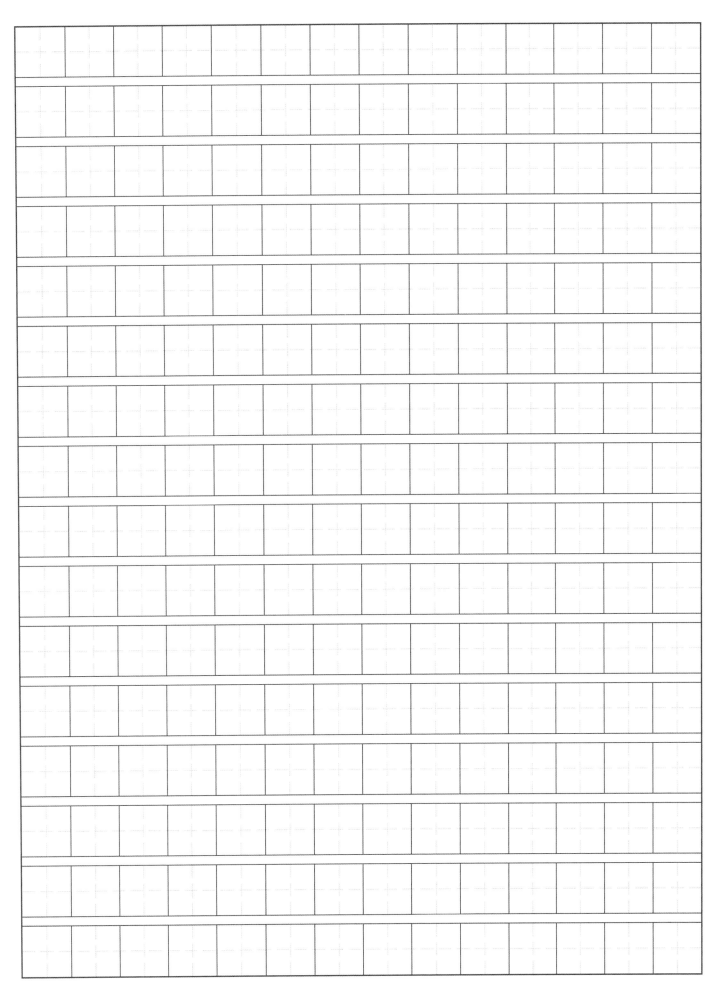

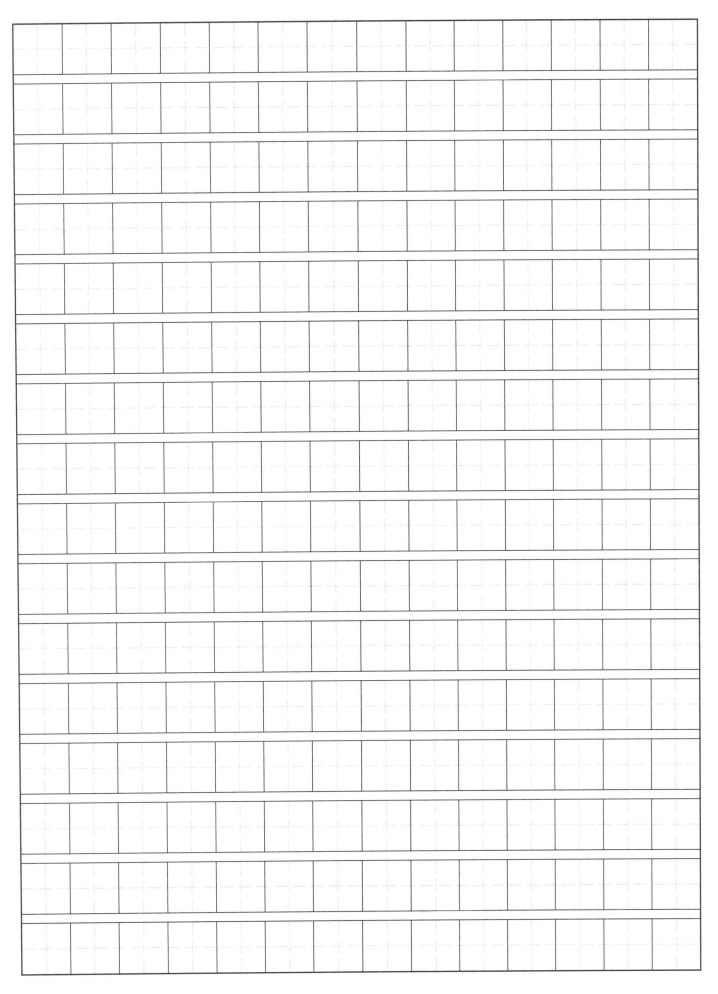

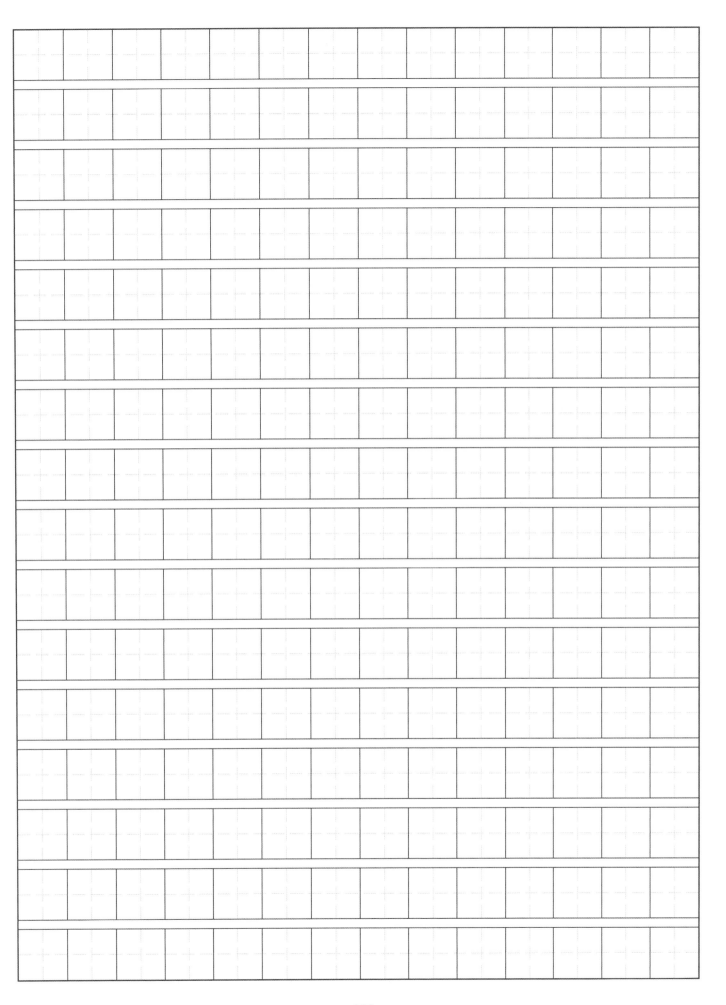

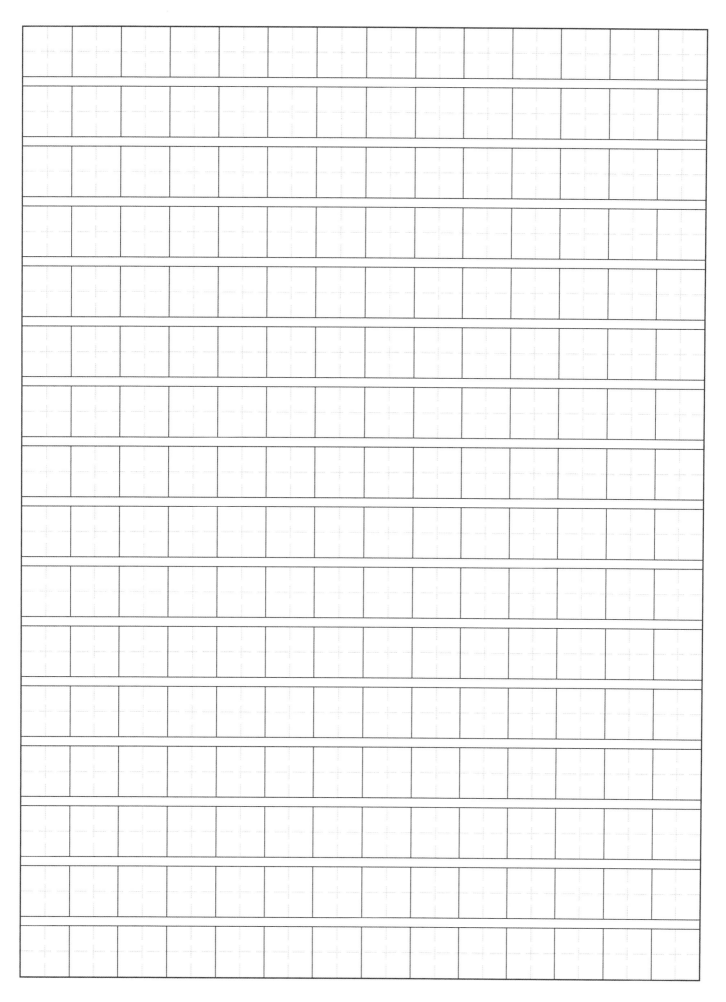

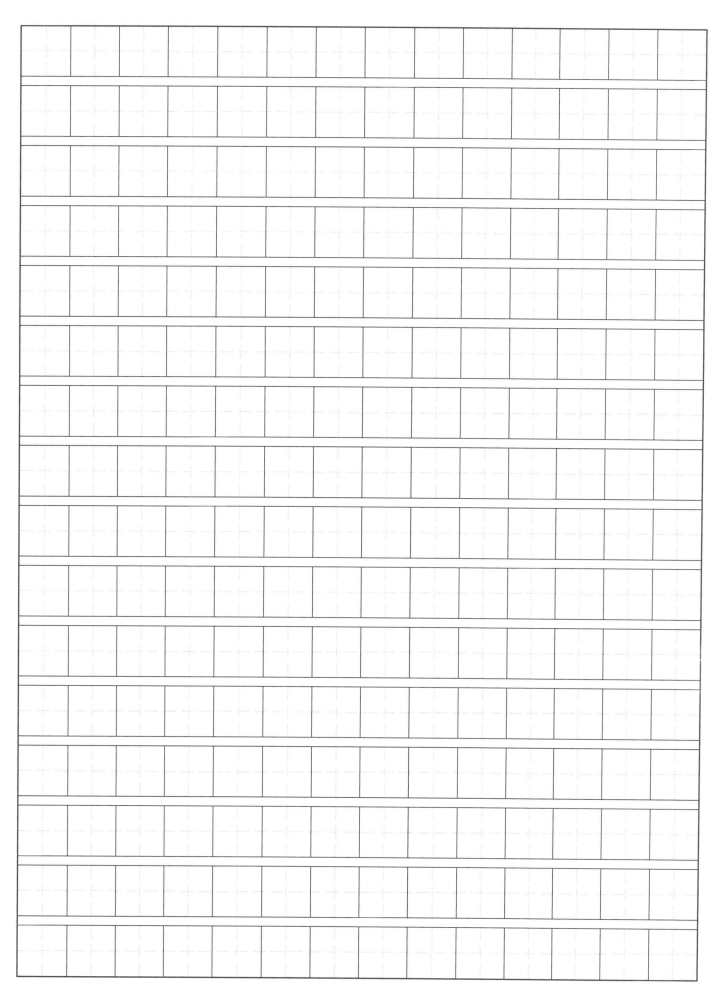

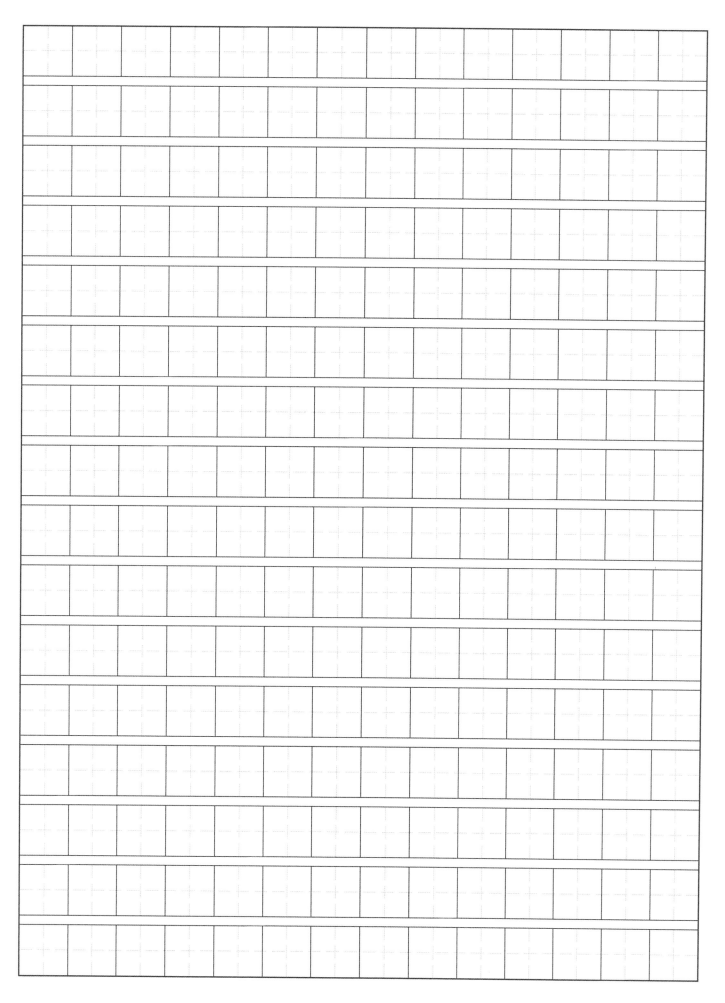

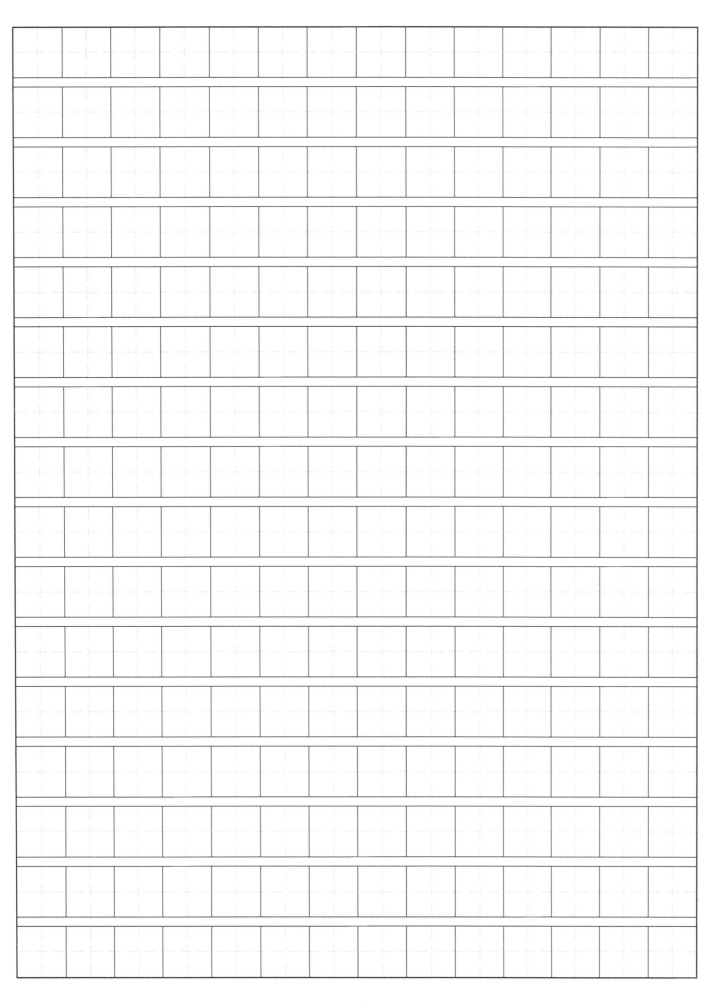

Chart Showing Consonant + Vowel Combinations

This chart shows the most commonly used consonants and vowels of the Hangeul alphabet, and how they are combined to make syllables. The consonants are on the left axis of the chart and the vowels are along the top. The combinations are shown in the table.

Vowels / Consonants	ㅏ a	ㅑ ya	ㅓ eo	ㅕ yeo	ㅗ o	ㅛ yo	ㅜ u	ㅠ yu	ㅡ eu	ㅣ i
ㄱ g	가 ga	갸 gya	거 geo	겨 gyeo	고 go	교 gyo	구 gu	규 gyu	그 geu	기 gi
ㄴ n	나 na	냐 nya	너 neo	녀 nyeo	노 no	뇨 nyo	누 nu	뉴 nyu	느 neu	니 ni
ㄷ d	다 da	댜 dya	더 deo	뎌 dyeo	도 do	됴 dyo	두 du	듀 dyu	드 deu	디 di
ㄹ l (r)	라 la	랴 lya	러 leo	려 lyeo	로 lo	료 lyo	루 lu	류 lyu	르 leu	리 li
ㅁ m	마 ma	먀 mya	머 meo	며 myeo	모 mo	묘 myo	무 mu	뮤 myu	므 meu	미 mi
ㅂ b	바 ba	뱌 bya	버 beo	벼 byeo	보 bo	뵤 byo	부 bu	뷰 byu	브 beu	비 bi
ㅅ s	사 sa	샤 sya	서 seo	셔 syeo	소 so	쇼 syo	수 su	슈 syu	스 seu	시 si
ㅇ silent	아 a	야 ya	어 eo	여 yeo	오 o	요 yo	우 u	유 yu	으 eu	이 i
ㅈ j	자 ja	쟈 jya	저 jeo	져 jyeo	조 jo	죠 jyo	주 ju	쥬 jyu	즈 jeu	지 ji
ㅊ ch	차 cha	챠 chya	처 cheo	쳐 chyeo	초 cho	쵸 chyo	추 chu	츄 chyu	츠 cheu	치 chi
ㅋ k	카 ka	캬 kya	커 keo	켜 kyeo	코 ko	쿄 kyo	쿠 ku	큐 kyu	크 keu	키 ki
ㅌ t	타 ta	탸 tya	터 teo	텨 tyeo	토 to	툐 tyo	투 tu	튜 tyu	트 teu	티 ti
ㅍ p	파 pa	퍄 pya	퍼 peo	펴 pyeo	포 po	표 pyo	푸 pu	퓨 pyu	프 peu	피 pi
ㅎ h	하 ha	햐 hya	허 heo	혀 hyeo	호 ho	효 hyo	후 hu	휴 hyu	흐 heu	히 hi
ㄲ kk	까 kka	꺄 kkya	꺼 kkeo	껴 kkyeo	꼬 kko	꾜 kkyo	꾸 kku	뀨 kkyu	끄 kkeu	끼 kki
ㄸ tt	따 tta	땨 ttya	떠 tteo	뗘 ttyeo	또 tto	뚀 ttyo	뚜 ttu	뜌 ttyu	뜨 tteu	띠 tti
ㅃ pp	빠 ppa	뺘 ppya	뻐 ppeo	뼈 ppyeo	뽀 ppo	뾰 ppyo	뿌 ppu	쀼 ppyu	쁘 ppeu	삐 ppi
ㅉ jj	짜 jja	쨔 jjya	쩌 jjeo	쪄 jjyeo	쪼 jjo	쬬 jjyo	쭈 jju	쮸 jjyu	쯔 jjeu	찌 jji
ㅆ ss	싸 ssa	쌰 ssya	써 sseo	쎠 ssyeo	쏘 sso	쑈 ssyo	쑤 ssu	쓔 ssyu	쓰 sseu	씨 ssi

Everyday Korean Vocabulary

These pages list key vocabulary words that often appear in the TOPIK test and are also useful for everyday conversations. Each word is given in English, Hangeul script and romanized Korean.

Personal Information
(TRACK 14)

personal information	개인정보	gaeinjeongbo
address	주소	juso
age	나이	nai
birthday	생일	saengil
cellphone number	휴대전화 번호	hyudaejeonhwa beonho
date of birth	생년월일	saengnyeonwolil
driver's license	운전면허증	unjeonmyeonheojeung
hometown	고향	gohyang
ID card	신분증	sinbunjeung
marriage	결혼	gyeolhon
nationality	국적	gukjeok
occupation	직업	jikeop
passport	여권	yeogwon
phone number	전화 번호	jeonhwa beonho
school	학교	hakkyo
single	미혼	mihon
married	기혼	gihon
divorced	이혼	ihon

People & Families
(TRACK 15)

person	사람	saram
family	가족	gajok
mother	어머니	eomeoni
mom	엄마	eomma
father	아버지	abeoji
dad	아빠	appa
parents	부모님	bumonim
sister	자매	jamae
brother	형제	hyeongje
daughter	딸	ttal
son	아들	adeul
grandmother	할머니	halmeoni
grandfather	할아버지	halabeoji
granddaughter	손녀	sonnyeo
grandson	손자	sonja
cousin	사촌	sachon
wife	아내	anae
husband	남편	nampyeon
adult	어른	eoreun
child	어린이	eorini
woman	여자	yeoja
man	남자	namja
friend	친구	chingu

Countries, Nationalities, Languages
(TRACK 16)

country	나라	nara
foreign country	외국	oeguk
nationality	국적	gukjeok
language	언어	eoneo
Korea	한국	hanguk
Korean nationality	한국인	hangukin
Korean language	한국어	hangukeo
foreigner	외국인	oegukin
foreign language	외국어	oegukeo
Britain	영국	yeongguk
British nationality	영국인	yeonggukin
English language	영어	yeongeo
America	미국	miguk
American nationality	미국인	migukin
Australia	호주	hoju

Australian nationality	호주인	hojuin
Germany	독일	dokil
German nationality	독일인	dokilin
German language	독일어	dokileo
China	중국	jungguk
Chinese nationality	중국인	junggukin
Chinese language	중국어	junggukeo
Japan	일본	ilbon
Japanese nationality	일본인	ilbonin
Japanese language	일본어	ilboneo

Pop Culture
(TRACK 17)

all-kill	올킬	olkil
awesome	대박	daebak
celebrity	연예인	yeonyein
clapping	박수	baksu
content	내용	naeyong
culture	문화	munhwa
director	감독	gamdok
fan	팬	paen
fan chant	응원	eungwon
fan club	팬클럽	paenkeulleop
fandom	팬덤	paendeom
fan service	팬서비스	paenseobiseu
hater fan	안티팬	antipaen
idol	아이돌	aidol
K-pop	케이팝	keipap
lyrics	가사	gasa
main character	주인공	juingong
music video	뮤직 비디오	myujik bidio
pop song	가요	gayo
singer	가수	gasu
soap opera	드라마	deurama
song	노래	norae
stalker fan	사생팬	sasaengpaen
title	제목	jemok
variety show	예능	yeneung
writing music	작곡	jakgok

IT & Social Media
(TRACK 18)

app	앱	aeb
computer	컴퓨터	keompyuteo
data	데이터	deiteo
download	다운로드	daunrodeu
email	이메일	imeil
Facebook	페이스북	peiseubuk
Instagram	인스타그램	inseu ta geulaem
Internet	인터넷	inteonet
laptop	노트북	noteubuk
login	로그인	logeuin
logout	로그아웃	logeuaut
password	패스워드	paeseuwodeu
selfie	셀카	selka
social media	소셜미디어	sosyeol midieo
smartphone	스마트폰	seumateupon
software	소프트웨어	sopeuteuweeo
tablet	테블렛	taebeullet
text message	문자	munja
Twitter	트위터	teuwiteo
Tweet	트윗	teuwit
YouTube	유튜브	yutubeu

Numbers

Korean has two number systems: Native numbers and Sino numbers. Native numbers go from 1–99 and are for counting and ages. Sino numbers are used for phone numbers, addresses, dates, money and numbers above 100.

Native Numbers

1	하나	hana
2	둘	dul
3	셋	set
4	넷	net
5	다섯	daseot
6	여섯	yeoseot
7	일곱	ilgop
8	여덟	yeodeol
9	아홉	ahop
10	열	yeol
11	열하나	yeolhana
12	열둘	yeoldul
13	열셋	yeolset
14	열넷	yeolnet
15	열다섯	yeoldaseot
16	열여섯	yeolyeoseot
17	열일곱	yeolilgop
18	열여덟	yeolyeodeol
19	열아홉	yeolahop
20	스물	seumul
21	스물하나	seumulhana
22	스물둘	seumuldul
23	스물셋	seumulset
24	스물넷	seumulnet
25	스물다섯	seumuldaseot
26	스물여섯	seumulyeoseot
27	스물일곱	seumulilgop
28	스물여덟	seumulyeodeol
29	스물아홉	seumulahop
30	서른	seoreun
31	서른하나	seoreunhana
32	서른둘	seoreundul
40	마흔	maheun
42	마흔둘	maheundul
50	쉰	swin
53	쉰셋	swinset
60	예순	yesun
64	예순 넷	yesun net
70	일흔	ilheun
80	여든	yeodeun
90	아흔	aheun

Sino Numbers

0	공	gong
1	일	il
2	이	i
3	삼	sam
4	사	sa
5	오	o
6	육	yuk
7	칠	chil
8	팔	pal
9	구	gu
10	십	sip
11	십일	sipil
12	십이	sipi
13	십삼	sipsam
14	십사	sipsa
15	십오	sipo
16	십육	sipyuk
17	십칠	sipchil
18	십팔	sippal
19	십구	sipgu
20	이십	isip
21	이십일	isipil
22	이십이	isipi
23	이십삼	isipsam
24	이십사	isipsa
25	이십오	isipo
26	이십육	isipyuk
27	이십칠	isipchil
28	이십팔	isippal
29	이십구	isipgu
30	삼십	samsip
31	삼십일	samsipil
40	사십	sasip
50	오십	osip
60	육십	yuksip
70	칠십	chilsip
80	팔십	palsip
90	구십	gusip
100	백	baek
1000	천	cheon

Telling Time

1 o'clock	한 시	han si
2 o'clock	두 시	du si
3 o'clock	세 시	se si
4 o'clock	네 시	ne si
5 o'clock	다섯 시	daseot si
6 o'clock	여섯 시	yeoseo si
7 o'clock	일곱 시	ilgop si
8 o'clock	여덟 시	yeodeolp si
9 o'clock	아홉 시	ahop si
10 o'clock	열 시	yeol si
11 o'clock	열 한 시	yeol han si
12 o'clock	열 두 시	yeol du si
1:15	한 시 십오 분	han si sipo bun
2:30	두 시 삼십 분 / 반	du si samsip bun/ban
3:45	세 시 사십오 분	se si sasipo bun

Days of the Week

Monday	월요일	wolyoil
Tuesday	화요일	hwayoil
Wednesday	수요일	suyoil
Thursday	목요일	mokyoil
Friday	금요일	geumyoil
Saturday	토요일	toyoil
Sunday	일요일	ilyoil

Months

January	일월	ilwol
February	이월	iwol
March	삼월	samwol
April	사월	sawol
May	오월	owol
June	유월	yuwol
July	칠월	chilwol
August	팔월	palwol
September	구월	guwol
October	시월	siwol
November	십일월	sipilwol
December	십이월	sipiwol

Days of the Month

1st	일 일	il il
2nd	이 일	i il
3rd	삼 일	sam il
4th	사 일	sa il
5th	오 일	o il
6th	육 일	yuk il
7th	칠 일	chil il
8th	팔 일	pal il
9th	구 일	gu il
10th	십 일	sip il
11th	십일 일	sipil il
20th	이십 일	isip il
21st	이십일 일	isipil il
30th	삼십 일	samsip il
31st	삼십일 일	sapsipil il

Basic Verbs

to be	이다	ida
to not be	아니다	anida
to have	있다	itta
to not have	없다	eopsda
to arrive	도착하다	dochakhada
to ask	묻다	mutda
to attend	다니다	danida
to borrow	빌리다	billida
to buy	사다	sada
to cancel	취소하다	chwisohada
to choose	고르다	goreuda
to close	닫다	datda
to close (one's eyes)	감다	gamda
to come	오다	oda
to decide	정하다	jeonghada
to depart	출발하다	chulbalhada
to dislike	싫어하다	sileohada
to do	하다	hada
to drink	마시다	masida
to eat	먹다	meokda
to exercise	운동하다	undonghada
to explain	설명하다	seolmyeonghada
to find	찾다	chatda
to forget	잊다	itda
to give	주다	juda
to go	가다	gada
to go in	들어가다	deuleogada
to go out	나가다	nagada
to go to work	출근하다	chulgeunhada
to graduate	졸업하다	joleophada
to help	돕다	dopda
to introduce	소개하다	sogaehada
to invite	초대하다	chodaehada
to know	알다	alda
to not know	모르다	moreuda
to laugh	웃다	utda
to learn	배우다	baeuda
to leave work	퇴근하다	toegeunhada
to like	좋아하다	joahada
to live	살다	salda
to lose	잃다	ilta
to love	사랑하다	saranghada
to make	만들다	mandeulda
to marry	결혼하다	gyeolhonhada
to meet	만나다	mannada
to open	열다	yeolda
to open (one's eyes)	뜨다	tteuda
to order	주문하다	jumunhada
to play	놀다	nolda
to promise	약속하다	yaksokhada
to put (sth in)	넣다	neota
to put (sth on)	두다	duda
to read	읽다	ilkda
to receive	받다	batda
to ride	타다	tada
to run	뛰다	ttwida
to see	보다	boda
to sell	팔다	palda
to sing	노래하다	noraehada
to sleep	자다	jada
to speak	말하다	malhada
to speak on the phone	통화하다	tonghwahada
to start	시작하다	sijakhada
to study	공부하다	gongbuhada
to talk	대화하다	daehwahada
to teach	가르치다	gareuchida
to think	생각하다	saenggakhada
to touch	만지다	manjida
to travel	여행하다	yeohaenghada
to use	사용하다	sayonghada
to wait	기다리다	gidarida
to wake up	일어나다	ileonada
to walk	걷다	geotda
to wash	씻다	ssisda
to work	일하다	ilhada
to write	쓰다	sseuda

Adjectives

bad	나쁘다	nappeuda
beautiful	아름답다	aleumdapda
boring	지루하다	jiruhada
cheap	싸다	ssada
clean	깨끗하다	kkaekkeuthada
close	가깝다	gakkapda
cold (to touch)	차갑다	chagapda
convenient	편리하다	pyeonlihada
cool-looking	멋있다	meosissda
cute	귀엽다	gwiyeopda
dangerous	위험하다	wiheomhada
dark	어둡다	eodupda
difficult	어렵다	eoryeopda
dirty	더럽다	deoreopda
easy	쉽다	swipda
expensive	비싸다	bissada
famous	유명하다	yumyeonghada
far	멀다	meolda
fast; early	빠르다	ppareuda
friendly	친절하다	chinjeolhada
good	좋다	jota
hard; firm	단단하다	dandanhada
heavy	무겁다	mugeopda
hot (to touch)	뜨겁다	tteugeopda
interesting	재미있다	jaemiitta
new	새롭다	saeropda
noisy	시끄럽다	sikkeureopda
old	낡다	nakta
pretty	예쁘다	yeoppeuda
quiet	조용하다	joyonghada
safe	안전하다	anjeonhada
slow; late	느리다	neurida
soft	부드럽다	budeureopda
strong	강하다	ganghada
weak	약하다	yakhada
young	젊다	jeomta

Adverbs

again	다시	dasi
a little	조금	jogeum
all	모두	modu
almost all	대부분	daebubun
already	벌써	beolsseo
always	항상	hangsang
early	일찍	iljjik
first	첫 / 처음	cheot / cheoeum
how	어떻게/얼마나	eotteoke / eolmana
later	나중에	najunge
more	더	deo
the most	최고	choego
most	제일	jeil
never	전혀	jeonhyeo
(not) very much	별로	byeollo
(not) at all	전혀	jeonhyeo
occasionally	종종	jongjong
often; very well	자주	jaju
perhaps	아마	ama
quick, promptly	어서	eoseo
really	정말	jeongmal
shortly	금방	geumbang
sometimes	가끔	gakkeum
too	너무	neomu
usually	보통	botong
very	아주	aju
yet	아직	ajik

Basic Grammar Tips

KOREAN WORD ORDER AND SPEECH STYLES

In Korean, the main verb or adjective comes at the end of a sentence while the other elements such as the subject and object appear before the verb or adjective. The word order is made clear by particles that are attached to the nouns. The word order within the sentence is flexible, as long as the verb or adjective retains the final position. In addition, the subject of the verb is usually not mentioned in Korean if it is understood from the context.

Korean sentence word order:	Subject	Object	Verb
	나는	아침을	먹어요
	naneun	achimeul	meokeoyo
	I	*breakfast*	*eat*

Koreans use different speech styles depending on the relationship between the speakers, the setting, the topic, etc. The polite speech style using sentence endings 어요 / 아요 **eoyo / ayo**, is commonly used in daily conversations. These polite endings are used for both questions and statements and sometimes even for suggestions and commands.

THE USE OF NOUN PARTICLES

Particles are attached to the end of nouns to indicate the function of these nouns as well as to add meanings to them, as prepositions do in English.

The subject particles 이 / 가 **i / ga**
이 / 가 **i / ga** are particles that indicate the subject of a sentence. The particle 이 **i** is used when the subject noun ends in a consonant, whereas 가 **ga** is used when the subject noun ends in a vowel.

> 학생이 와요.
> Haksaeng**i** wayo.
> *A student comes.*

> 날씨가 좋아요.
> Nalssi**ga** joayo.
> *The weather is good.*

The topic particle 은 / 는 **eun / neun**
은 / 는 **eun / neun** are particles that emphasize the topic of a sentence. The particle 은 **eun** is used when the topic noun ends in a consonant, whereas 는 **neun** is used when the topic noun ends in a vowel.

> 마이클은 미국 사람이에요.
> Maikeul**eun** miguk saramieyo.
> *Michael is American.*

> 나는 한국 사람이에요.
> Na**neun** hanguk saramieyo.
> *I am Korean.*

The object particle 을 / 를 **eul / reul**
을 / 를 **eul / reul** are particles that indicate the object of a sentence. The particle 을 **eul** is used when the object noun ends in a consonant, whereas 를 **reul** is used when the object noun ends in a vowel.

> 나는 아침을 먹어요.
> Naneun achim**eul** meokeoyo.
> *I eat breakfast.*

> 사라가 커피를 마셔요.
> Saraga keopi**reul** masyeoyo.
> *Sarah drinks coffee.*

The locative particle 에 / 에서 **e / eseo**
에 **e** indicates a place and location. When 에 is attached to verbs such as 가다 **gada** *to go*, 오다 **oda** *to come* and 다니다 **danida** *to attend*, it indicates one's destination. 에서 **eseo** is used to indicate the location of an activity.

> 집에 있어요.
> Jip**e** isseoyo.
> *I am at home.*

> 집에 가요.
> Jip**e** gayo.
> *I am going home.*

> 집에서 공부해요.
> Jip**eseo** gongbuhaeyo.
> *I am studying at home.*

The time particle 에 **e**
에 **e** indicates the time when an action takes place.

> 아침에 일어나요.
> Achim**e** ileonayo.
> *I wake up in the morning.*

> 한 시에 만나요.
> Han si**e** mannayo.
> *Let's meet at one o'clock.*

The possessive particle 의 ui
의 **ui** indicates ownership.

나의 시계예요.
Na**ui** sigyeyeyo.
It is my watch.

스티븐의 핸드폰이에요.
Seutibeun**ui** haendeuponieyo.
It is Steven's cellphone.

The recipient particles 한테 / 에게 hante / ege
한테 / 에게 **hante / ege** indicates the receiver of an item or a beneficiary of an action. 한테 **hante** is usually used in everyday spoken language whereas 에게 **ege** is used in formal speech or written language.

케이트가 친구한테 꽃을 줘요.
Keiteuga chingu**hante** kkocheul jwoyo.
Kate gives a flower to her friend.

The animate source particles 한테서 / 에게서 hanteseo / egeseo
한테서 / 에게서 **hanteseo / egeseo** are used to mark the source of an action, when the source is animate (i.e., a person or animal). 한테서 **hanteseo** is usually used in spoken language whereas 에게서 **eygeseo** is used in formal settings or written language.

친구한테서 선물을 받았어요.
Chingu**hanteseo** seonmuleul batasseoyo.
I received a gift from a friend.

The companion particles 하고 and 와 / 과 hago and wa / gwa
하고 and 와 / 과 **hago** and **wa / gwa** are used to link two nouns, like "and" in English. 하고 **hago** is usually used in spoken language whereas 와 / 과 **wa / gwa** are used in formal speech or in written language. 와 **wa** is used when the noun ends in a vowel, whereas 과 **gwa** is used when the noun ends in a consonant.

물하고 주스 주세요.
Mul**hago** juseu juseyo.
Please give (me) water and juice.

사과와 빵을 먹어요.
Sagwa**wa** ppangeul meokeoyo.
(I) eat an apple and bread.

책상과 의자가 있어요.
Chaeksang**gwa** uijaga isseoyo.
There is a desk and chair.

The instrument particle (으)로 (eu)ro
(으)로 **(eu)ro** indicates the instrument with which an action is performed. Nouns ending with ㄹ combine with 로 **ro**, not 으로 **euro**. Note **ro** can be romanized as **lo**.

펜으로 쓰세요.
Pen**euro** sseuseyo.
Please write with a pen.

영어로 말하세요.
Yeongeo**ro** malhaseyo.
Please speak in English.

연필로 쓰세요.
Yeonpil**lo** sseuseyo.
Please write with a pencil.

The inclusive particle 도 do
도 **do** is used to add an item or object to another in a list, like "also" or "too" in English.

컴퓨터가 있어요. 노트북도 있어요.
Keompyuteoga isseoyo. Noteubuk**do** isseoyo.
I have a computer. I also have a laptop.

The exclusive particle 만 man
만 **man** indicates one thing to the exclusion of all others.

우리 가족은 미국에 살아요. 저만 한국에 살아요.
Uri gajokeun miguke salayo. Jeo**man** hanguke salayo.
My family lives in America. Only I live in Korea.

The particles expressing starting and ending 부터 and 까지 buteo and kkaji
부터 and 까지 **buteo** and **kkaji** are attached to time or place nouns to indicate the start or end of a situation.

아홉 시부터 다섯 시까지 일해요.
Ahop si**buteo** daseos si**kkaji** ilhaeyo.
I work from 9 to 5.

BASIC SENTENCE PATTERNS

Basic sentence patterns in Korean are as follows.

Equating two things N1 은 / 는 N2 이에요 / 예요
[N1 eun / neun N2 ieyo / yeyo]
This pattern is used to express that the first noun N1 equates to the second noun N2. When N2 ends in a consonant, the particle 이에요 **ieyo** is attached to it, whereas 예요 **yeyo** is used when it ends in a vowel.

나는 한국 사람이에요.
Na**neun** hanguk saram**ieyo.**
I am Korean.

브랜든은 의사**예요**.
Beuraendeun**eun** uisa**yeyo**.
Brendan is a doctor.

Negative expressions N1 은 / 는 **N2** 이 /
가 아니에요 **N1 eun / neun N2 i / ga anieyo**

This pattern is used to express that two things are not the same.

나는 중국 사람**이 아니에요**.
Na**neun** jungguk saram**i anieyo**.
I am not Chinese.

엘렌은 기자**가 아니에요**.
Ellen**eun** gija**ga anieyo**.
Ellen is not a reporter.

Expressing possession N 이 / 가 있어요 / 없어요
i / ga isseoyo / eopseoyo

This pattern is used to express the possession of an item or person.

가방**이 있어요**.
Gabang**i isseoyo**.
(I) have a bag.

친구**가 없어요**.
Chingu**ga eopseoyo**.
(I) don't have a friend.

BASIC VERB TENSE ENDINGS

To talk about the present, past or future, the following verb endings are used. The subject of a verb is often omitted in Korean.

Present tense verb endings 어요 / 아요 **eoyo / ayo**

These verb endings are used to make statements or ask questions in the present tense.

한국어 공부를 하시**어요**.
Hangukeo gonbureul hasie**oyo**.
(One is) studying Korean.

한국어 공부를 하시**어요**?
Hangukeo gonbureul hasie**oyo?**
Are you studying Korean?

한국어를 알**아요**?
Hangukeoreul al**ayo**?
Do you know Korean?

Past tense verb endings 었어요 / 았어요 / ㅆ어요
eosseoyo / asseoyo / sseoyo. These verb endings are used to make statements or ask questions in the past tense. When the verb ends in a consonant, 었어요/았어요 **eosseoyo / asseoyo** are used whereas ㅆ어요 **sseoyo** is used when it ends in a vowel.

아침을 먹**었어요**.
Achimeul meok**eosseoyo**.
(I) had breakfast.

아침을 먹**었어요**?
Achimeul meok**eosseoyo?**
Did (you) eat breakfast?

전화를 받**았어요**.
Jeonhwareul bat**asseoyo**.
(I) received a phone call.

애나는 독일에 **갔어요**.
Aennaneun dokile **gasseoyo**.
Anna went to Germany.

Future tense verb endings (으)ㄹ 거예요 **(eu)l geoyeyo**

These verb endings are used to make statements or ask questions about a likely future. When the verb stem ends in a consonant, the ending 을 거예요 **eul geoyeyo** is used. When the verb stem ends in a vowel, ㄹ 거예요 **-l geoyeyo** is used. When ㄹ **l** is at the end of the verb stem, 으 **eu** is omitted.

책을 읽**을 거예요**.
Chaekeul ilk**eul geoyeyo**.
(I) will read a book.

책을 읽**을 거예요**?
Chaekeul ilk**eul geoyeyo?**
Will (you) read a book?

서점에 **갈 거예요**.
Seojeome **gal geoyeyo**
(I) will go to a bookstore.

USING ADJECTIVES IN SENTENCES

Adjectives in Korean are conjugated in the same way as verbs and use the same endings to express the present, past or future tense. So essentially, adjectives are considered to be a type of verb in Korean.

숙제가 많**아요**.
Sukjega man**hayo**.
(I have) lots of homework.

꽃이 예**뻐요**.
Kkochi ye**ppeoyo.**
The flower is pretty.

점심이 맛있**었어요**.
Jeomsimi masiss**eosseoyo.**
The lunch was delicious.

상자가 작**았어요**.
Sangjaga jak**asseoyo.**
The box was small.

지난 주는 바**빴어요**.
Jinan juneun ba**ppasseoyo.**
(I) was busy last week.

내일 날씨가 좋**을 거예요**.
Naeil nalssiga jo**eul geoyeyo.**
Tomorrow's weather will be good.

NEGATIVES OF VERBS AND ADJECTIVES

The negatives 안 an and 못 mos

안 **an** is used for general negation of an action or state. 못 **mos** is used when external circumstances prevent a person from doing something. 안 **an** or 못 **mos** are placed immediately before the verb or adjective.

수영장에 **안** 가요.
Suyeongjange **an** gayo.
(I'm) not going to the swimming pool.

오늘 **안** 바빠요.
Oneul **an** bappayo.
(I am) not busy today.

자전거를 **못** 타요.
Jajeongeoreul **mos** tayo.
(I) cannot ride a bike.

"Books to Span the East and West"

Tuttle Publishing was founded in 1832 in the small New England town of Rutland, Vermont [USA]. Our core values remain as strong today as they were then—to publish best-in-class books which bring people together one page at a time. In 1948, we established a publishing office in Japan—and Tuttle is now a leader in publishing English-language books about the arts, languages and cultures of Asia. The world has become a much smaller place today and Asia's economic and cultural influence has grown. Yet the need for meaningful dialogue and information about this diverse region has never been greater. Over the past seven decades, Tuttle has published thousands of books on subjects ranging from martial arts and paper crafts to language learning and literature—and our talented authors, illustrators, designers and photographers have won many prestigious awards. We welcome you to explore the wealth of information available on Asia at www.tuttlepublishing.com. at **www.tuttlepublishing.com**.

Published by Tuttle Publishing, an imprint of Periplus Editions (HK) Ltd.

www.tuttlepublishing.com

Copyright © 2020 by Periplus Editions (HK) Ltd.
Pages 1–9 by Tina Cho.
Pages 121–127 courtesy of Woojoo Kim.

ISBN 978-0-8048-5328-6

TUTTLE PUBLISHING® is a registered trademark of Tuttle Publishing, a division of Periplus Editions (HK) Ltd.

Distributed by

North America, Latin America & Europe
Tuttle Publishing
364 Innovation Drive
North Clarendon, VT 05759-9436 U.S.A.
Tel: 1 (802) 773-8930 Fax: 1 (802) 773-6993
info@tuttlepublishing.com www.tuttlepublishing.com

Asia Pacific
Berkeley Books Pte. Ltd.
3 Kallang Sector #04-01
Singapore 349278
Tel: (65) 6741 2178 Fax: (65) 6741 2179
inquiries@periplus.com.sg www.tuttlepublishing.com

25 25 24 23 22
10 9 8 7 6 5 4

Printed in Singapore   2112TP